*Building Customer and Employee*

# ALLEGIANCE

*Building Customer and Employee*
# ALLEGIANCE

Paul R. Timm, Ph.D.

A Publication of

**COMMUNICATION SOLUTIONS**

# Building Customer and Employee Allegiance

Paul R. Timm, Ph.D.
© 2004 Paul R. Timm

## Communication Solutions

1165 N. 1100 East
Orem, Utah 84097
801 426-4678

## Quantity Discounts and Customized Printings

This book is available at special quantity discounts when purchased in bulk by your corporation, organization, or group. Special imprints, messages, and excerpts can be produced to meet your needs. For more information, contact the author:

801 426-4678
DrTimm@aol.com
www.DrTimm.com

ISBN 0-9745562-1-1

Printed and bound in the United States of America

# Contents

# Preface

al·le·giance / n / :
the obligation of support . . .
loyalty to or support for a person,
cause, or organization . . .

Customer and employee allegiance may well be your company's greatest asset. Such allegiance has more impact on the bottom line than any ad campaign, marketing program, or employee-relations initiative.

Turned-off employees and irritated customers produce devastating ripple effects that drag companies into a morass of mediocrity or worse. The cost of replacing lost customers quickly dissipates any of the benefits gained from offering quality products, using clever and effective advertising, or implementing cutting-edge marketing. The cost of replacing or re-motivating disengaged employees or distributors saps organizational energy and resources.

The alternative to building allegiance is to constantly scramble to replace the inevitably lost customers or workers—and to repair the damage done to the bottom line. The oft-quoted statistic that it costs five times as much to get a new customer than it does to keep an existing one may be conservative in today's technology-enabled economy. Likewise, statistics showing employee-turnover costs ranging from 25 to 150 percent of the employees' salaries underscore how employee defections eat profits.

How bad is the problem of customer and employee churn? It varies, of course, but by reliable estimates, one customer in four is dissatisfied with some aspect of a business transaction. Such dissatisfaction sows the seeds for loss, especially for companies that fail to systematically earn customer allegiance. Employee turnover in the U.S. is about 12 percent across the board. Again, some companies face much higher numbers; some do better.

The seeds of opportunity lie nestled within these rather dismal statistics. Companies that succeed at improving customer allegiance dramatically boost their profitability. A 5-percent increase in customer retention can yield between 25-percent and 100-percent increases in profits across a variety of industries, according to Fredrick Reichheld in *Loyalty Rules!* (Harvard Business School Press, 2001).

This book offers straight talk about building the allegiance of your customers and employees. It offers you a powerful and easy-to-employ approach that virtually guarantees results. It is based on sound theory, but it is written as easily applicable tactics. The approach does not rely on chance or luck. It provides the tools and direction needed to build a solid foundation for long-term growth and constant improvement. Such growth provides an exceptional competitive advantage.

I have intentionally kept this book concise and reader friendly. A few hours invested in these ideas will pay enormous dividends.

Your feedback is always appreciated. If you will share your experiences, comments, complaints, or questions with me, I will do my best to respond in a helpful manner. Email me at **DrTimm@aol.com** or visit **www.DrTimm.com**.

Thanks for reading this, and now let's explore ways for *Building Customer and Employee Allegiance.*

—Paul R. Timm, Ph.D.

# Chapter 1

# Getting Beyond Slogans and Good Intentions

**O**nly mismanagement of customer capital can explain why U.S. companies on average lose half their customers in five years, or why—despite obvious improvements in the quality of manufactured goods, negligible price increases, and unending rhetoric about treating customers right—customer satisfaction is actually declining in the United States.

—Thomas A. Stewart, *Intellectual Capital*

## The Way It Is . . .

The bank's billboards and television ads touted the slogan: "Currently giving 110%." When I asked a teller at my local branch what that meant, she looked at me with a blank stare and said, "I don't know. I just read the sign on my way to work." Does this bank value its customers? Are its employees on board with a coherent service strategy? It doesn't seem like it.

An upscale coffee shop had two people taking orders and money from the lines of customers waiting. But waiting was the true order of the day. After the customer's order was shouted out, the one young woman charged with actually producing the coffee concoctions was hopelessly bogged down and forced to labor amid widespread grumbling from customers who waited 20 minutes for their cup of java. Does this well-known coffee chain have good intentions to serve its customers? Of course. Did they show it? Not today.

A friend bought a television from a big-box electronics store. She got a good price and even sprang for the extended-warranty package. After one year, the TV developed the annoying habit of shutting down every 15 minutes. The repair technician came to her home but was unable to fix the television. He then took the set to the shop, where it lingered for three weeks, never, according to the repair people, exhibiting its quirky behavior. Returned to the customer, the set immediately resumed its narcolepsy.

Calls to the store resulted in endless debate about the fine points of the warranty with a man who claimed to be a customer service supervisor. In short, he wouldn't budge. He frequently put the customer on hold and came across as totally unsympathetic. The subtext of his message was, "I sure hope this woman just goes away." Well, good news. She did go away. And she took with her anyone who would listen to her report of endless wrangling over a television set.

The store spent more time and money stonewalling the customer than it would have cost to replace the defective set. For refusing to make good on a $270 television, it permanently lost this customer. Does the retailer have good intentions about customer service? I bet they say they do. Did they show it? Not to this customer.

I visited a well-known fast-food chain and found it strange that absolutely no one working there smiled. Their greetings were mechanical; the food delivery was prompt but unfriendly. Then it struck me: the manager (the only adult) labored with a grim determination. Her demeanor said that she ran a tight ship and that no frivolous behavior would be tolerated. The young employees conveyed all the charm of galley slaves. Does that fast-food chain want to send the message that employees are not to enjoy their work or that smiling is verboten? I don't think so. But that is the result it got—along with horrendous turnover of its employees.

## The Disconnect Between Service Intentions and Reality

What companies *say* about customer service often loses something in the translation of the message to employees. As a result, company intentions often bear little resemblance to what really happens. Do companies see this? And, if so, what do they do about it?

The first reaction of companies awakening to the need to improve allegiance is often to hire consultants or trainers to "motivate their people." They seem to think that a few pep talks can get their people fired up and make them love their jobs and love all their customers. I know this because I have been called on by numerous companies to perform this miracle. My training gigs are pretty entertaining. I get participants involved from the start; we toss out examples of service horror stories with wild abandon. We pinpoint the problems and list ideas for fixing them. After the sessions, we get new fire in the belly, we're ready to slay those bad-service dragons, and we're committed to kicking competitive butt. But then, within a few weeks, things are pretty much back to business as usual. The company thinks it gets points for providing employee training. Managers can display their good intentions—proof positive they are serious about giving good service. But intentions are not enough.

All companies have good intentions to be customer focused, employee friendly, and full of concern for their wonderful customers. Yet many have difficulty translating these good intentions into a formula for executing the intentions.

Fortunately, help is at hand. This book offers a clear and immediately applicable approach to earning the allegiance of customers and employees. With these ideas, any organization can create an ongoing engine for building customer and employee allegiance with all the economic benefits that accrue. But before we get to that, let's take a closer look at where companies go wrong—by faking it.

## How Companies Fake a Sincere Interest in Customer Service

Every company talks about giving great service, about how the customer is always right, the customer is the most important person, yada, yada. So why is it that companies on average lose half their customers in five years? Why—despite continuous improvements in the quality of manufactured goods, negligible price increases, and unending rhetoric about treating customers right—is customer satisfaction actually declining?

In a similar vein, every company wants to be a great place to work, to attract top talent, and to provide an outstanding work atmosphere. Yet employee turnover averages 12 percent a year across all industries and is much, much higher in some. Employees, like customers, vote with their feet and go to work in places they enjoy.

The reason ineffective companies lose customers and employees is that they don't really care; they just pretend to care. If they really cared, they wouldn't do so many dumb things. Here are eight ways companies create the illusion of caring, without spending a lot of time or effort. Companies fake it when they—

## 1. Keep service as a separate function or department

Companies that fake it set up a special department with complaint handlers who know all the tricks their customers might try to pull. They think this is what customer service is really all about.

These companies realize that having a separate department is more efficient than nurturing a culture in which everyone is equally responsible for serving customers and such service is recognized as the essence of their businesses.

## 2. Run customer service "programs"

Fake-it companies believe that service-improvement programs or special employee incentives must have a starting and ending point. After all, nothing goes on forever, right? They ignore the reality that customer-service efforts have no beginning and no end.

Of course, they could banish the word "program" and reinforce among employees that service must be an ongoing priority, a core strategy integral to everyone's success. But they don't.

## 3. Use one-shot training

Even worse than using "programs," fake-it companies hire high-priced, flashy speakers to get their people jazzed about customer service. This one-shot approach gives employees some new fire in the belly and gets them committed to kicking some competitive butt. Of course, the company doesn't bother to follow up this training, and, within a few weeks, things will be pretty much back to business as usual. The company gets points for providing employee training, and managers can cite these efforts as proof positive they are serious about giving good service. This is a great faking technique.

Of course, the company could use training as just one step in launching an ongoing strategy. The training could teach and motivate people in good service behaviors, empower them, reward their involvement, and launch ongoing processes for building customer loyalty. But faking it doesn't require any such tie-in.

## 4. Equate service with smilage

Fake-it companies know that smiling and being pleasant is all they really need to do to keep customers coming back. If customers have a problem or make an unusual request, they'll be sure their employees smile when they say, "That's not our policy."

Of course, they could also give employees the authority to fix things for customers; but when faking it, that would not be necessary. Just smile.

## 5. Rely on marketing tricks

Fake-it companies find that, instead of focusing on service, they can keep repeat customers with such gimmicks as frequent-flier programs or regular-diner discounts. They use incentives to hold customers (and employees) hostage. These incentive programs give customers an opportunity to overlook customer abuse and hate the company even more because they feel stuck with it.

Of course, such incentive deals hold customers only until a better offer comes along. Building a real and trusting relationship with customers works far better, but that requires effort and long-term commitment that fake-it companies won't give.

## 6. Flirt but never get married

Fake-it companies avoid *long-term commitment*. (Now there's a scary term. Can't we just be friends?) Of course, they can "just be friends" with customers and employees, as long as they don't mind constantly scrambling to replace the "friends" who went to competitors. Allegiance depends on ongoing, dare I say, *intimate* relationships with customers and employees. Locking in loyalty requires getting married—getting intimately involved in their needs and wants and creating a symbiotic relationship with them. But companies that prefer to fake it don't want to go to all that trouble.

## 7. Work hard to avoid complaints

Fake-it companies focus on *avoiding* complaints. They figure, the fewer complaints the better, right? Managers are rewarded for never getting a complaint—they become folk heroes in the company! Oh sure, some idealists argue that you actually want to hear from complaining customers so you can improve your service; but, hey, fake-it companies know that's bunk. They teach their employees to make it as difficult as possible for people to complain. Oh, and they never mention to their staff that for every one complainer there are likely to be a dozen customers with the same problem who never bring it up—but go to the competition instead.

Fake-it companies never buy that nonsense that complainers are really their best friends. They would never want to make it easy for people to give feedback, and they surely don't see a need to build allegiance by actually responding to customer and employee feedback.

## 8. Avoid measuring

While fake-it companies account for every penny and every tangible resource, they throw up their hands in futility when faced with measuring the impact of service efforts. After all, they figure they really can't measure such "soft" data as customer satisfaction, loyalty, and allegiance.

Conceptually, they agree that tracking data over time can help them know if they are improving, but they don't really want to know that—it might be embarrassing. It's much easier to fake a sincere interest in customer service and employee relations.

# How Company Efforts Can Go Wrong

Okay, so let's assume you are not a fake-it company and that you are sincere about earning the allegiance of customers and employees. Let's take a look at a few potential stumbling blocks, the most common of which are ambiguous goals, faulty assumptions about customers, ineffective systems, poor intervention attempts, and lack of measurement. Any of these problems can undercut even the best strategies.

## 1. Have fuzzy, ambiguous goals

For any organizational goal to work, it must be clearly defined and understandable to all who are working toward it. As described in the Preface of this book, I believe that *allegiance* is the ultimate goal. It reflects a sense of support, loyalty, and devotion to an organization. Customer and employee allegiance is created and enhanced when people experience three key elements:

- **Overall satisfaction.** Low or erratic levels of satisfaction disqualify the company for earning loyalty.

- **Commitment to make a sustained investment in an** *ongoing relationship* **with a company.** This commitment is manifest by an intention to be a repeat buyer or long-term participant and by resistance to switch to a competitor or another employer.

- **Willingness to recommend the company to others.** This willingness indicates that people are willing to "go public" in their support for the company and, in doing so, deepen their personal commitment to it.

When true customer allegiance emerges, relationships grow and ultimately become what Stephen Covey calls *customer synergy.* "Synergy," says Dr. Covey, "happens when both supplier and customer are changed by the experience, creating something new that neither knew about in the beginning. That experience creates a bonding. Nothing is as powerful as this bonding and, with it, you can leapfrog the competition."[1]

When a company builds customer allegiance using synergy, it is creating wealth in the form of *customer and employee capital*—the organization's intangible wealth that measures ultimate success. Customer capital has been defined as the value of a company's franchise, its ongoing relationship with the people or organizations to which it sells.[2] Companies best build such capital by earning people's allegiance. Allegiance is literally a form of wealth.

## 2. Work from faulty assumptions about customers

As we begin our process of earning customer and employee allegiance, let's take a look at some conventional wisdom—wisdom that may be off base. Forgive me if I slaughter a few sacred cows, but some overused axioms may be causing you or your people to miss the big picture. The following faulty assumptions can apply equally well to your employees (often called *internal customers*) as well as to your customers. Earning allegiance requires that we avoid buying into these oft-quoted but counterproductive ideas—

### Faulty assumption No. 1: "The customer is always right"

The intent of this slogan is probably fine, but by making one party always right, we implicitly set up the other party as wrong. The issue of rightness and wrongness is seldom relevant. Using such polar thinking—right versus wrong—precludes getting at the real issue of how we can build mutually useful relationships. If we are attempting to build a better marriage, do we say the husband (or wife) is always right? Of course not. When we instead look at the goal as being mutual satisfaction and relationship building, we don't have to choose sides.

If we insist that the customer is always right, then in every dispute the employee or company must be wrong. What kind of message is that? Who cares who's right or wrong? We're in business to fix problems, not to fix blame; to build relationships, not to choose sides.

## Faulty assumption No. 2: "Treat all customers the same"

Business isn't about democracy or the fairness of equal treatment. To paraphrase George Orwell's *Animal Farm*, all customers are equal but some are more equal than others.

The idea of treating all customers alike stems from a mass-marketing mindset. But today's successful businesses are less *mass* and more *individualized*, more "one-size-fits-*one*." They thrive on recognizing and dealing with individuals, each of whom is different. The blind pursuit of sheer numbers of customers or share of the market runs at cross purposes with the need to give the one-to-one, personalized service that lies at the heart of allegiance building and customer-capital formation. Treating all customers the same can be counterproductive. Some customers are simply more valuable than others.

A mass-marketing, treat-all-customers-the-same mindset explains all those credit-card applications we find in our mailboxes. Banks are so eager to increase their market shares that they overlook the fact that the average bank loses money on three out of five credit-card customers—those who use the card only occasionally and pay no interest.

Smart companies treat individual customers differently. Customers who have a greater impact on company success should be afforded special treatment not offered to less-profitable customers. Airline frequent-flyer programs, private bankers for high-income individuals, and organizations that give special incentives to elite customers are examples of not treating everyone equally. Companies that offer these kinds of unequal treatments are strengthening relationships with key profit-generating individuals.

Such special-treatment efforts should, of course, recognize long-term potential in customers who may not be currently profitable. As a board member of a credit union associated with a university, I see that many of our current customers (college students) are unprofitable to us—now. Typically these students have little savings and relatively small loan balances. They simply don't generate as much profit as do customers with larger incomes.[3] We still treat them well because we hope for a lifelong, and eventually profitable, relationship.

The best tactic is to treat elite customers special and motivate others to join your elite.

### Faulty assumption No. 3: "It takes big differences to build customer allegiance"

The most important underlying premise of any allegiance-building effort is that *little differences can have significant impact on customers.* People can purchase almost any product or service from several possible sources. They can work for several similar employers. The decision to go one place instead of another is a zero-sum game. The company either gets the customer or employee or it doesn't.

The customer's choice is almost always dependent on little things, seldom monumental differences. An unusually friendly clerk or co-worker, a slightly more convenient location, marginally quicker delivery, better packaging—any such things can push a person toward or away from the company. A major theme throughout this book is that *little things mean everything* and that attention to detail counts.

At the core of a customer-allegiance strategy is the notion that small, incremental improvements and little surprises given to customers and employees can pay enormous dividends. Once in place and actively managed, the approach described in this book will put your company ahead of the pack and pulling away.

## 3. Use ineffective systems

A third way companies go wrong in their quests for customer allegiance is in being unaware of the damaging effects of their company systems. The term *systems* often conjures up computers in people's minds, but I am using the term in a broader sense here. *Systems* refers to any aspect of organizational structure, processes, procedures, policies, or methods used to get the company's products to customers. Systems can range from store location to staffing adequacy, from employee training to telephone-call routing, from product guarantees to methods of packaging, and from employee rules to daycare assistance.

The worst systems problem arises when the company believes that service is a separate function or department. This separation tells employees that serving customers is not their main responsibility but is the responsibility of those guys in the customer-service department. It tells supervisors that employee relations are solely the function of the personnel office. Service can never be a separate department. Service is the *essence* of any business. Everyone is involved, not just one department or function.

## 4. Employ poor intervention attempts

Interventions are the efforts we make to change employee behaviors and organizational processes to maximize results. Training and development as well as organizational restructuring are examples of interventions.

Many companies initiate customer-service programs or campaigns aimed at improving some measures. But the description of customer service as a *program* or *campaign* implies a starting and ending point. Customer-service efforts have no beginning and no end. They are ongoing processes integral to any successful organization.

I recently did a series of training sessions for a medical clinic. The chief of staff expressed strong concern about patient satisfaction in an environment of increasing competition. I did workshops for all staff members and for the doctors. Following the sessions, I contacted the clinic manager to discuss follow-up. She listened to my reasoning but never did get around to scheduling additional implementation strategies. The result: very little was accomplished. The staff attempted to apply the ideas taught, but ideas faded and many went back to the old ways.

Too many companies use one-shot training. They hire a flashy speaker to get employees jazzed about customer service. They hold rallies or give great locker-room speeches and hope for the best. Of course, without follow-up, things quickly get back to normal.

Done correctly, training can be effective to launch an ongoing strategy. It can teach people service behaviors, empower them, reward their involvement, and initiate ongoing processes for building customer allegiance. But company efforts must have legs. The best interventions are ongoing and consistent, not disjointed special events.

## 5. Over-rely on marketing tricks or advertising

Advertising may bring a customer to you, but it has nothing to do with earning allegiance. In fact, traditional ads are not even all that good at bringing customers in. Experts looking at the future of advertising see a huge problem as customers try to cut through all the clutter. All the ad messages have become like wallpaper. They are everywhere, but no one really notices anymore. Some marketers say "companies may spend the next 1,000 years trying to cut through the clutter they created in the past 50."[4]

One axiom of marketing still passes the truth test: word-of-mouth is the best possible advertising. Loyal customers tell other people about good companies and products. This process is more powerful than the most elaborate mass-advertising campaign.

Attempts at buying allegiance with such things as repeat-customer programs, discounts, sales, or special deals may hold customers to a point, but only until a better marketing offer comes along. Companies need something more than marketing incentives to earn ongoing allegiance. A look at the airline mileage programs will show you that, while such programs get customers to stick with the airlines, overall satisfaction among passengers is dropping like a rock. These marketing incentive programs give customers an opportunity to hate their airlines more frequently.

Incentives can be helpful but are not a substitute for an ongoing customer-allegiance strategy.

## 6. Have a lukewarm commitment

Companies that behave like those I described in the chapter opening seem to have lukewarm commitment. Many companies do. Producing excellent service and creating customer allegiance are difficult tasks that require a huge commitment. If it were easy, every company would do it.

Lots of companies want to flirt with their customers but never build real relationships or engage in the customer synergy that forges alliances and long-term commitment. Without loyal customers, your efforts will necessarily focus on constantly scrambling to replace the customer who went to your competitors.

The commitment must come from the heart of the organization. It must be rooted in corporate values and culture; it must be at the forefront of every employee's mind. This is no small challenge. It requires an unwavering commitment.

## 7. Fail to measure

The final common failing of company customer-service efforts is failure to measure the results of their efforts. The irony of this is astounding. Companies that account for every penny and every tangible resource throw up their hands in futility when faced with measuring the impact of service efforts. You *must* measure the impact of service efforts.

Different organizations will choose to measure different things. But ultimately, the company needs to know to what degree it is earning the allegiance of its customers and employees. It must actively listen and process the feedback it receives to measure effectiveness. Often such measures must rely on "soft" data, but this is no reason to discount their importance.

The simplest way to assess overall customer and employee allegiance is to get answers to the three critical questions that get at the essence of allegiance—

1. **How satisfied are you?**

2. **Do you intend to keep doing business with us?**

3. **Would you recommend us to a friend?**

Additional questions that address specific areas of company concern can be added to these, but don't overburden the respondents with too many.

Some organizations solicit these answers from every customer. For example, an auto dealership asks customers to fill out a card with these three questions while they wait to ring up their purchases at the service department.

Many companies are going to the use of a Web-based dialoguing system that asks people to respond to these questions while it also gives them opportunities for providing other feedback to the company. I will get into more detail about this in Chapter 3 and show how your organization can apply an active-listening process for measuring key variables.

Getting a good, consistent sample and tracking that data over time can tell a great deal about allegiance-building efforts. Data (whether soft or hard) can and must be measured.

## The Payoff for Learning Allegiance

The payoff for using the approach described in this book will be the enhancement of customer and employee capital—your organization's greatest assets. The strategy and tactics you will learn from this book grow out of a value-chain model that assesses—

- the customers' and employees' experiences,

- their responses to those experiences,

- the impact of those responses on the creation of allegiance, and

- the creation of customer capital—organizational wealth—as personified by high-allegiance customers and employees.

The remainder of this book fleshes out this value-chain model. It considers the experiences of customers and employees in—

- Avoiding typical service turnoffs (value, system, and people problems) (Chapter 2).

- Experiencing and dealing with recovery efforts as problems arise (Chapter 3).

- Receiving service that exceeds their expectations (Chapters 4-8).

- Recognizing the value in managing and sustaining the process for continuous improvement (Chapter 9).

# Empowering and Energizing Employees

Earning customer allegiance and creating customer capital is a team sport. It requires coordinated effort and *esprit de corps*. It requires some risk taking—some willingness to fail and learn from failures. It requires the courage to solicit and use feedback—even when such feedback may be painful.

Every organizational stakeholder can and should play this team sport. The benefits arising from active involvement in ongoing service improvement accrue both to the organization and to the individuals who participate.

Participants in the strategy-implementation process will experience a sense of accomplishment and growth. They will see the impact and share in the satisfaction of a job well done. In today's tight labor markets, such fulfillment at work can be an important way to hold onto key players. Energized employees beget healthy, successful organizations.

# Committing to Continuous Quality Improvement

The approach described in this book assumes that today's actions can always be improved on, that the bar is constantly being raised, and that as companies achieve higher levels of service quality, they strengthen their distinctive competencies.

Continuous quality improvement makes it prohibitively expensive for competitors to imitate your level of competence. The more difficult you become to imitate, the stronger your competitive position.

The approach described in this book is simple—not necessarily easy, but simple. It calls for the consistent application of specific tactics within the context of active dialoguing, participative management, and a dynamic organizational climate.

The following chapters will teach you the tactics for taking your company far beyond slogans and good intentions, as you earn customer and employee allegiance.

Applying these tactics will create in the minds of your customers and employees a positive sense of *allegiance*—obligation, support, loyalty, and even devotion to your organization. A company can have no greater asset.

## Notes

1. Stephen Covey, "Customer Synergy," *Customer Service Management*, Jan/Feb 2000, p. 66.

2. This definition is attributed to Hubert Saint-Onge in Thomas A. Stewart, *Intellectual Capital: The New Wealth of Organizations*, (New York: Doubleday/Currency, 1997), p. 143.

3. Credit unions are not-for-profit and member-owned financial institutions, providing financial services for "the little guy." The credit union movement began in the 1930s when common people found they were generally ignored by banks. Some people argue that the same situation exists today.

4. Jonathan Kaufman, "The Omnipresent Persuaders," *Wall Street Journal*, January 1, 2000, p. R26.

# Chapter 2

# Identifying Customer and Employee Turnoffs

The single most important thing to remember about any enterprise is that results exist only on the outside. The result of a business is a satisfied customer. Inside an enterprise, there are only costs.

—Peter Drucker, *The New Realities*[1]

## The Way It Is . . .

On a recent cross-country trip, my tire blew out on the Ohio Turnpike south of Toledo. It was 6 p.m. on Friday, the temperature hovered in the upper 90s, and traffic was heavy. The right rear tire blew like a bomb, and I limped onto the median to dodge the constant flow of rumbling semis. I called the American Automobile Association's hot line on my cellphone. I was greeted by an unsympathetic monotone who mechanically sought my membership card number, expiration date, address, home phone, complete description of my car, my mother's maiden name, and the middle name of my oldest grandchild or some such stuff. All the while I am attempting to explain to her the imminent danger of being crushed by a big rig roaring by at 80 mph.

"Exactly where are you?" she asked. I tried to explain my general location. That wasn't good enough. I'd need to give her an exact mileage marker. So I trekked up the median in 98-degree heat, screaming into the cellphone over the roar of the trucks, until I could see a mileage marker. She then told me that a tow truck would be there "in 45 minutes or less" and that I was to jump out of the car when I saw him coming to flag him down. This, apparently, so that he would know *which* white Lexus with a blown-out tire in the median at mileage marker 68 of the Ohio Turnpike was mine.

Fifty minutes later I called for an update. "Any possibility that the truck will actually get here today?" I asked. A different, and more sympathetic, service rep answered this time; and after going through the membership card info all over again, he told me he would "check to see *if they'd received my call!*" I waited on hold for four minutes. I was not encouraged. He then, to his credit, at least apologized ("I'm sorry about the wait. The truck was called to an accident up the road.") and promised me the truck would be there in "25 minutes or less." I waited.

This story has a happier ending. The truck driver—Paul, it said on his shirt—was a very nice man. He immediately apologized and told me he was literally 50 miles away when he got the call. He then jumped to work on my tire and I was on the road again. I also had a pleasant surprise: my newly purchased car had a full-size spare tire mounted on a matching wheel. I was anticipating one of those crummy emergency donuts and a trip to the tire store before I could continue my travel. Thank you, Lexus!

Paul was a lifesaver. If I had attempted to change the tire myself, I would have lost it when discovering the special socket for the locking lug nuts. Paul knew his stuff, and I somehow felt secure in the shadow of his huge towing rig. We chatted pleasantly and he worked efficiently and, although the "45 minutes or less" turned out to be an hour and 18 minutes, I was saved as a Triple-A customer by a tow-truck operator named Paul from Toledo, Ohio.

But there were moments when AAA ran a serious risk of losing me, a customer since 1984. Paul's behavior overcame the indifferent telephone behaviors of the AAA employees. And Lexus moved me one step toward customer allegiance by providing a real spare tire.

## What Turns Customers Off?

Winning a war requires knowing the enemy. Tactic No. 1 in our quest to earn customer and employee allegiance is to know what turns people off. What kinds of things can lead to a serious risk of losing a customer, partner, associate, or employee—perhaps forever?

My twelve years of research in customer allegiance began with the question, What turns customers off? In one study (with my colleague, Dr. Kristen B. DeTienne), we gathered open-ended responses to that question. Our content analysis of almost two thousand collected comments identified three categories of customer turn-offs that disqualify organizations from earning allegiance: value, systems, and people. The data reveal that the following ten turn-offs accounted for 97 percent of all comments cited by the participants of the study:[2]

### Value turnoffs

- Poor guarantee or failure to back up products
- Quality not as good as expected
- Price too high for value received

## Systems turnoffs

- Slow service, or help not available
- Business place dirty, messy, or cluttered
- Low selection or poor availability of product
- Inconvenient location, layout, parking, or access

## People turnoffs

- Lack of courtesy, friendliness, or attention
- Employees who lack knowledge or are not helpful
- Employee appearance or mannerisms

Follow-up interviews and further study seems to confirm that these categories provide a useful framework for identifying root causes of customer dissatisfaction. Let's look at each in more depth and see how these can also apply to employee dissatisfaction.

# Value Turnoffs Make Customers Feel Shortchanged

Customers experience a value turnoff when they feel shortchanged on the quality, quantity, reliability, or appropriate "fit" of a product or service.

Feeling shortchanged is a function of what someone expects. Expectations are influenced by the cost of the goods or services. Customers don't expect the same thing from a low-cost item as they do from more costly ones. But when characteristics of the core product fail to live up to what customers anticipate, they experience value turnoffs.

A quick example: Suppose you have a 79-cent ballpoint pen that quits writing. You may be momentarily annoyed, but you'll throw it away and get another pen. But if the pen that quits cost you $79 instead of 79 cents, you will be much more than momentarily annoyed. Likewise, a $5 fast-food lunch that wasn't so good will be soon forgotten, while a $50 dining experience of poor quality will trigger a much more severe reaction.

The responsibility for reducing value turnoffs lies with top leadership in a company. Executive management is ultimately responsible for determining the nature of the products sold. Selling cheap goods may be a perfectly acceptable strategy so long as customers recognize that quality cannot be expected to be as good as a higher-priced alternative. Leaders must determine if they want to be a Mercedes or a Hyundai, Nordstrom's or K-mart, a full-service bank or a post-dated-check or quick-loan business. Any of these decisions may be fine so long as pricing and perceived value reflects the quality of the products.

Many companies choose a low-cost-provider strategy. Some stores sell only products that cost less than a dollar. Warehouse retailers stack it deep and sell it cheap. This may be a legitimate business strategy and can be profitable. But a company that purports to provide higher-quality products and some semblance of service needs to be certain that customer expectations are being met or exceeded. Companies providing inadequate value are soon discovered and soon out of business.

In the arena of *employee* satisfaction, companies may also seek long-term, high-quality relationships with their employees or they may simply accept high worker turnover as a given. Some excellent companies that choose the former approach expend considerable resources and effort in making employees feel valued. Some companies go to great lengths, for example, to minimize the need for layoffs when economic conditions force cutbacks. Some avoid even using the term "layoff," instead citing occasional needs to "lay aside" employees only until the economy permits re-hiring them. While lifetime-employment guarantees are rarely a realistic expectation, high-value companies invest in their people, build employee skills with excellent training, provide exceptional work facilities, foster healthy corporate cultures, and strive to re-ward employee allegiance with company allegiance to them.

## Systems Turnoffs Inconvenience Customers

Systems turnoffs arise from the way a company delivers its products or services. This entails a wide range of factors ranging from product selection, business location, policies and procedures, customer convenience and comfort efforts, staffing, employee training, and, of course, technology systems as well. As you can imagine, systems problems include a multitude of sins.

When transactions are unnecessarily complicated, inefficient, or troublesome for people as customers or employees, they experience systems turnoffs. Complaints about long lines, slow service, poor selection, untrained employees, workplace appearance, and poor signage are examples of systems problems.

I recently experienced a rather strange systems turnoff with Icelandic Airlines. I was told by an airline representative to confirm my return flight 48 hours before flying home. Although I had flown to Iceland six times in the past year, I had never been told to do that before. I dutifully called the airline two days before my flight and was met with a phone menu that did not include a selection for confirming flight reservations. I finally selected another choice and, after being on hold for about a minute (while I got to listen to the airline's advertisements), I was connected to a person. The representative sounded a little surprised that I was actually reconfirming my flight! I got the strong impression that this call was totally unnecessary, and I felt mildly embarrassed that I had done what the company claimed I was required to do.

A recent study by Jupiter Communications, an e-commerce monitoring firm, looked at a common practice among online retailers that creates annoyance for customers: requiring Website visitors to register and provide personal information before they can browse or buy. Jupiter's study concluded that 40 percent of online users are deterred from using sites that require such registration. Microsoft's Expedia Web travel business decided to drop that requirement. Expedia marketing VP Erik Blachford said, "When you walk into a department store, clerks don't ask for your name and password before letting you shop."[3] A common online procedure has become a systems turnoff for many customers.

My research shows that the No. 1 turnoff for many customers is slow service. In hundreds of training sessions I have conducted across the U.S. and in Europe, I ask people to identify their pet peeves about customer service. In virtually every group, one of the first things cited is slow service or having to wait. We live in a society that values speed and efficiency and that resents things that slow us down.

Company systems determine the speed of service because they involve staffing, layout of the business, accessibility, efficiency of delivery, employee relations policies, and so on. The responsibility for implementing and maintaining effective systems lies with a company's management, because changes in systems almost always require spending money. A company's decision to add personnel, provide additional training, change locations, implement new delivery methods, or even rearrange the office layout will require management approval.

Employees who lack the knowledge to answer customer questions and organizations that have just one person capable of fulfilling a key function are symptoms of systems failures. Telephone menus that are unnecessarily complicated (dial 1 for such and such, 2 for so and so, etc.) are another common turnoff described by customers. Poor location, lack of delivery options, cluttered workplace, clumsy or repetitive paperwork requirements, lack of parking, and poor selection as a result of inadequate reordering processes are additional examples of systems problems for both customers and employees.

# People Turnoffs Make Customers Feel Discounted

People turnoffs arise when employees who represent the company project inappropriate behaviors, indifferent attitudes, or mechanical tone. People turnoffs include such things as rudeness, poor nonverbal behaviors such as lack of eye contact, inappropriate dress and grooming, autocratic bosses, and any behaviors that convey a low level of caring or consideration for others.

Responsibility for reducing people turnoffs lies with every employee. Often people are unaware of how their behaviors communicate. Training can help raise awareness, but ultimately the individual staff member will decide how he or she will interact with customers and other employees.

Because teaching specific behaviors is often difficult, hiring people with good attitudes and interpersonal skills is especially important. Some successful employers constantly recruit people they experience in other customer situations. Communication training can help in raising awareness and teaching suggested ways of phrasing comments to customers.

People communicate the way they do because they have learned that behavior. Changes come slowly and only with considerable effort. The best way to change communication behavior is by raising awareness, modeling new behaviors, having people try the new behavior, and reinforcing the improvement. Companies can benefit from using scripts or scripted phrases and from clearly identifying communication taboos—certain messages, terms, and nonverbal behaviors that are unacceptable.

Here is a brief description of the three turnoff categories as applied to my road-trip experience:

| *Value* Turnoffs | Had paid my dues for years and never used AAA's road service before. Was not sure I was getting a good deal. |
|---|---|
| *Systems* Turnoffs | Policy of saying "45 minutes or less" to me was initially reassuring, but when the deadline was not met, it was a turnoff. Required much information before allowing me to explain my problem. |
| *People* Turnoffs | Unsympathetic tone of voice, no expressions of empathy. |

In the case of my Ohio road trip, factors that initially turned me off (tone of voice, uncaring attitude, demands for information, and inaccurate promises about response time) were mitigated by the good service of a dedicated employee, the truck driver who was personable, friendly, and reassuring. He worked with expertise and efficiency.

And that is largely the point of this discussion. Turnoffs happen. By recognizing and categorizing them, companies can assign responsibility and attack them. The other tactics presented in this book show ways to mitigate the negative effects of such turnoffs.

# Reducing Turnoffs Is the Best Advertising

No company can succeed if it lets turnoffs aggravate its customers to the point where they quit doing business with it. A typical company will lose 10 percent to 30 percent of its customers each year because it turned them off. This touches off a treadmill-like scramble to replace the lost customers with new customers—an effort- and cost-intensive process. Employee turnover is often a result of turnoffs as well. A far more efficient process is to keep and build upon the current customer base.

Customer and employee allegiance is like an election held every day, and people vote with their feet. If dissatisfied, they walk (sometimes run) to a competitor. When customers cannot realistically switch to another company (in the case of a public utility or government agency, for example) they use their feet for something else: they kick back with anger or animosity directed toward the organization and its employees. When employees cannot move on to better companies, they produce shoddy work, undermine their supervisors, aggravate their co-workers, and create all sorts of mischief and counterproductive activity.

Many people think that it is advertising that induces people to buy. U.S. businesses spend about $11.5 billion a year on advertising. Yet surveys show that only 25 percent of those polled say that a television ad would induce them to buy. Likewise, only 15 percent and 13 percent respectively said that newspaper or magazine ads caused them to buy. In short, traditional advertising has little confidence among consumers. Ads can create awareness, of course, but they alone rarely make people buy.

Advice or the recommendation from a friend or relative, however, scored 63 percent as a determinant of people buying a new product.[4] This confirms what people have long known: Word of mouth is still the best way to attract customers.

To sustain repeat business, a company must generate positive word-of-mouth by reducing the turnoffs and exceeding customer expectations. People talk to others about a service experience when it is exceptional or out of the ordinary. Bad news travels faster and further than good news. A company can have the best products available, but if it fails to minimize customer turnoffs and provide a positive customer experience, few people will notice the difference between that company and its competition. We will talk a lot more about exceeding expectations in later chapters.

# The Cost of the Lost Customer

Some employees don't understand the real cost of a lost customer. When an unhappy customer decides to stop doing business with a company, the costs are almost always more than people realize. To get a clearer view of the cost impact of a lost customer, I want to use an example of a business we are all familiar with: a grocery supermarket. Here's a story of "Mrs. Williams":

Harriett Williams, a sixty-something single woman, has been shopping at Happy Jack's Super Market for many years. The store is close to home and its products are competitively priced. Last week, Mrs. Williams approached the produce manager and said, "Sonny, can I get a half head of lettuce." He looked at her like she was deranged and curtly said, "Sorry, lady. We just sell the whole head." She was a bit embarrassed but accepted his refusal.

Later she had several other small disappointments (she wanted a quart of skim milk and they had only half gallons), and when she checked out her groceries she was largely ignored by the clerk, who was carrying on a conversation with another employee. The clerk made matters worse by abruptly demanding two forms of ID with Harriett's check ("What do they think I am, a common criminal?" thought Mrs. Williams) and by failing to say thank you.

Mrs. Williams walked out of the store that day and decided that she was no longer going to shop there. Although she had been a Happy Jack's customer for many years, she realized that Happy Jack's employees couldn't care less if she shopped there. She had been spending about fifty hard-earned dollars there every week, but that was going to change. She felt that, to the store employees, she was just another cash cow to be milked without so much as a sincere thank you. Nobody cared whether she was a satisfied customer.

What do the employees think about that? They're not worried. Life is like that. You win some; you lose some. Happy Jack's is a big chain and doesn't really need Mrs. Williams. Besides, she can be a bit cranky at times, and her special requests are stupid. (Who ever heard of buying a half head of lettuce!) They'll survive without her $50 a week. Too bad she's unhappy, but a big company like this can't twist itself into contortions just to save one little old lady from going down the street to the competition. Look at the bottom line. After all, it can hardly be considered a major financial disaster to lose one little customer like Mrs. Williams. Or can it?

The employees at Happy Jack's need to understand some economic facts of life. Successful businesses look at the ripple effects of their service, not just at the immediate profit from an individual purchase.

The shortsighted employee sees Mrs. Williams as a small customer dealing with a big company. Let's change that view: look at the situation from another, broader perspective.

The loss of Mrs. Williams is not, of course, merely a $50 loss. It's much, much more. She was a $50-a-week buyer. That's $2,600 a year or $26,000 over a decade. (Perhaps she would have shopped at Happy Jack's for a lifetime, but we will use the more conservative ten-year figure for illustration.) But that's only the tip of the iceberg lettuce.

Ripple effects make it much worse. Studies show that an upset customer tells on average between ten and twenty other people about an unhappy experience. Some people will tell many more, but let's stay conservative and assume that Mrs. Williams told eleven. The same studies say that these eleven may tell an average of five others each. This could be getting serious!

How many people are likely to hear the bad news about Happy Jack's? Look at the math:

| Mrs. Williams | 1 person |
|---|---|
| tells eleven others | +11 people |
| who each tell five | +55 people |
| Total who heard = | **67 people** |

Are all 67 of these people going to rebel against Happy Jack's? Probably not. Let's assume that of these 67 customers or potential customers, only one-quarter of them decide not to shop at Happy Jack's. Twenty-five percent of 67 (rounded) is 17.

Assuming that these 17 people would also be $50-a-week shoppers, Happy Jack's stands to lose $44,200 a year, or $442,000 in a decade, because Mrs. Williams was upset when she left the store. Somehow, giving her that half head of lettuce doesn't sound so stupid.

Although these numbers are starting to get alarming, they are still conservative. In many parts of the country, a typical supermarket customer spends $100 or more a week, so losing a different customer could quickly double the figures of Mrs. Williams' case.

Customer-service research says that it costs at least five times as much to attract a new customer (mostly advertising and promotion costs) as it does to keep an existing one (where costs may include giving refunds, offering samples, replacing merchandise, or giving a half head of lettuce). One report put these figures at about $19 to keep a customer happy versus $118 to get a new buyer into the store.

Again, some quick math shows the real cost of the lost Mrs. Williams:

| | |
|---|---|
| Cost of keeping Mrs. Williams happy | $19 |
| Cost of attracting 17 new customers | $2,006 |

Now let's make our economic facts of life even more meaningful to each employee.

Lost customers can mean lost jobs. The Robert Half Organization, a well-known personnel consulting firm, shows a simple way to calculate the amount of sales needed to pay employee salaries. Assuming that a company pays 50 percent in taxes and earns a profit of 5 percent after taxes, Table 1 shows how much must be sold to pay each employee (in four different salary levels) and maintain current profit levels:

| Table 1. Sales Needed to Sustain a Job | | | |
|---|---|---|---|
| Salary | Benefits | After-Tax Cost | Sales Needed |
| $40,000 | $18,400 | $29,200 | $584,000 |
| $25,000 | $11,500 | $18,250 | $365,000 |
| $15,000 | $6,900 | $10,950 | $219,000 |
| $10,000 | $4,600 | $7,300 | $146,000 |

These figures will vary, of course. But the impact on one's job can be clearly shown.

If a $10,000-a-year part-time clerk irritates as few as three or four customers in a year, the ripple effects can quickly exceed the amount of sales needed to maintain that job. Unfortunately, many organizations have employees who irritate three or four customers a day!

On the employee-relations front, the costs are similarly disturbing. If a company ignores the need to maintain employee allegiance, it incurs enormous costs from unproductive workers and turnover. Human-resources consultants cite costs of at least 150% of a person's base salary to replace him or her. And, the more the company pays a person, the higher that percentage will be—because the more it pays this person, obviously, the more it values his or her contribution to the growth and success of the business. Most businesses will probably pay their top salesperson triple (or more) what they pay a bookkeeper. The business values the contributions of the salesperson at a higher level, at least in strictly monetary terms, over those of the bookkeeper, although both perform valuable roles.

If an employee with an annual salary of $50,000 feels badly treated and leaves a company, and if the company plans to replace that person, the costs can be a minimum of $75,000. The business costs associated with employee turnover arise from four major categories:

- Costs due to a person leaving (severance pay, continuation of benefits, moving expenses, etc.)
- Costs of hiring a replacement (advertising the job, processing applications, interviewing, etc.)
- Costs of training (to teach the new employee his or her job)
- Costs of lost productivity (while the new employee is brought up to speed).

Knowing the turnoffs faced by employees as well as by customers can be invaluable. Look at your company through their eyes, and consistently work to identify values, systems, and people turnoffs that may affect your bottom line.

Awareness of the costs of customer and employee turnoffs leads to the inevitable conclusion that organizations must be proactive in dealing with those turnoffs. The remaining chapters of this book describe workable tactics any company can take to minimize the damage inflicted by turnoffs. For starters, you must develop or refine your systems for recovering the potential lost customer or employee. Chapter 3 focuses on such recovery techniques.

## Notes

1. Peter Drucker, *The New Realities* (New York: Harper Collins, 1989), p. 6.

2. Paul R. Timm and Kristen B. DeTienne, "How Well Do Businesses Predict Customer Turnoffs?: A Discrepancy Analysis," *Journal of Marketing Management,* Vol. 5, No. 2, 1997.

3. Frank Barnako, "Expedia Drops Registration," *InfoBeat,* an online newsletter sponsored by CBS MarketWatch, January 4, 2000.

4. Bernice Johnson, President, Milestone Unlimited, Inc., Portland, Oregon, in a letter to the editor, Fast Company, April-May, 1998, p. 32.

# Chapter 3

# Recovering Dissatisfied Customers and Employees

> Those who enter to buy, support me. Those who come to flatter, please me. Those who complain, teach me how I may please others so that more will come. Those only hurt me who are displeased but do not complain. They refuse me permission to correct my errors and thus improve my service.
>
> —*Retailing pioneer Marshall Field*

## The Way It Is . . .

Sherri went to her local supermarket. It was a busy afternoon, she was tired from working all day, and the store was busy. At the checkout, the clerk let an apple slip out of the plastic bag and drop to the floor. The clerk started to put it back in the bag and Sherri said, "Hold it. I don't want an apple that's been on the floor." The clerk said "You can go back to the produce department and get another one." Sherri didn't want to delay the line any more and was too tired to go do that.

Josh, a young man who was bagging groceries at the next counter, overheard this conversation and immediately said, "I'll get you another apple." As he jogged off to the produce department, Sherri apologized to the people behind her in line. She was about to tell the clerk to just skip it, when Josh came back, panting slightly, and handed her a beautiful apple, saying, "Sorry for the delay." He then brought his other hand from behind his back and added, "And here's another one for your inconvenience."

Timo's favorite eatery is Pop's Café. Located a few blocks from his downtown office, Pop's has the best home cooking, complete with fresh-baked biscuits. The owner of the restaurant (yup, his nickname is actually Pop) personally greets each customer, and the food is delicious. One day, as Timo paid for his meal, Pop asked if everything was okay. Timo half-jokingly mentioned that the biscuits weren't as warm as usual. The owner immediately handed his money back. Timo tried to pay him, saying the meal was fine, just not quite as great as it usually is. But Pop would hear nothing of this and refused to accept payment. Timo continues to be a regular customer and frequently introduces his friends and business associates to Pop's.

A tiny, almost insignificant gesture reconfirmed in Sherri's mind that her grocery store is the place she wants to shop. A restaurant owner's demonstration that he wants only 100 percent satisfied customers strengthened Timo's allegiance to Pop's Café.

Hearing and addressing customer complaints is a crucial tactic in building customer allegiance. And, as with so many things today, e-commerce has turbo-charged this process. Organizations have several options for collecting customer feedback, some of which are more effective than others. We'll look at some of these options in this chapter, but the prerequisite to choosing a method is that companies must genuinely want to receive feedback—even when it may be uncomfortable. The best companies jump at opportunities to hear from their customers, especially the complaining ones.

# Service Glitches Are Opportunities

Any company can give adequate customer service when everything goes well. A smooth transaction is easy. But when glitches occur—when customers have problems or are even a little bit disappointed—the great companies quickly distinguish themselves.

Recovering potentially lost customers or employees is best accomplished when companies see it as an opportunity rather than a painful chore. Granted, most of us would prefer to not hear about customer or employee dissatisfaction. That's human nature. But given that dissatisfaction is inevitable, smart managers see the recovery process as an opportunity and a challenge. Complaints pose opportunities to cement relationships. The vast majority of customer and employee relationships are worth saving, although occasionally—I stress *occasionally*—you may need to let go of the chronic complainer, as I'll discuss later in this chapter.

Your business is very likely to experience some customers who have unrealistic expectations of the products and services you have committed to deliver. These expectations may be the result of a misunderstanding from previous experiences, or they may be the result of a customer's chronic (and unrealistic) demand for value at your expense. When these customers demand far more than you can profitably deliver, you have several choices:

- negotiate for the delivery of the expected products and services,
- deliver your products and services as part of the original agreement, or
- terminate the relationship with the customer.

Whichever route you choose, you create an opportunity to evaluate potential improvements as a result of the feedback you receive. I'll talk more about such feedback in a moment. But first, let's look at some interesting facts revealed in surveys by the U.S. Office of Consumer Affairs:

- One customer in four is dissatisfied with some aspect of a typical transaction.

- Only 5 percent of dissatisfied customers complain to the company. The vast silent majority would rather switch than fight. They take their business elsewhere.

- A dissatisfied customer, on average, will tell 12 other people about a company that provided poor service.

Let's translate those statistics: If 25 percent of you customers are unhappy with some aspect of your company's service but only 5 percent of that 25 percent bother to complain (yet each unhappy customer tells a dozen others) the impact can be devastating. For simplicity, let's say a company serves 100 customers a day. Twenty-five of them are dissatisfied, but the company hears only one or two complaints. That may sound good to management until they realize that the 23 quiet ones are likely to tell 274 other people about the unsatisfactory service!

Just as I illustrated in the Happy Jack's Supermarket example in Chapter 2, the ripple effects can be devastating. Only by being open to complaints or concerns can companies turn this lemon into lemonade. Hearing customer and employee complaints is the first and most crucial step in fixing problems and maintaining allegiance. You really must *want* to hear from people, and you really must make it easy for people to give you feedback. Avoiding feedback is, as someone once said, like being an ostrich. An ostrich can bury its head, but he always leaves the other end exposed.

Although this may sound counterintuitive, enlightened companies can and should increase the number of complainers they hear from. Handling complaints from two or three dissatisfied people can save 30 or 40 possible defections. And these complaints can teach the company what it needs to know to improve.

The best news of all is that customers who have their complaints handled well are very likely to do business with the company again. While only 9 to 37 percent of dissatisfied customers who don't complain report a willingness to do business with the company again, fully 50 to 80 percent of those whose complaints are dealt with will consider doing repeat business—even if their complaints were not resolved in their favor.[1] Other findings put this number even higher.

When an organization creates a dialoguing process with customers and employees, those who participate can become the company's best friends—even when complaining. To make the most of such dialoguing, you need to—

- Make it easy for people to voice complaints (as well as compliments, suggestions, and questions).

- Act on input quickly and efficiently.

# Make It Easy for Customers to Complain

Dissatisfaction happens. What we choose to do about it can make all the difference in creating customer and employee allegiance. To do something about dissatisfaction, we need to know when it is happening—we need to get the silently dissatisfied customer to speak up by creating open communication channels.

Open communication occurs best when people feel that their opinions are valued and that they will be rewarded (or at least not punished) for expressing them. Companies earn allegiance by participating in dialogue. Dialoguing can be greatly enhanced with an easy-to-use feedback system.

Most people find expressing a complaint to be an unpleasant experience. It's uncomfortable and a bit intimidating. Most people want to maintain cordial relationships and fear that complaining will upset others. Our job, then, is to let people know that we are sincerely open to their comments—negative or positive. Below are a few ways to make this process more effective.

## Seek input at the point of contact

Most companies have some sort of formal feedback system, ostensibly to gather data that could make service better. These systems can show historical trends and even measure customer allegiance rates, if well designed. But the information they provide is often too little, too late, and too broad-brush. The time to gain specific, useful insights from an unhappy customer is at the point of contact and at the time of the problem.

For a rapidly growing number of people, the Internet (or, within many companies, an intranet) provides the easiest way to give feedback. Some people prefer direct communication with organization employees, the telephone, or letters. Creating a climate in which people will give real-time, on-the-spot feedback is almost always more effective than printed customer-feedback cards, telephone follow-ups, or focus-group sessions.

## Reinforce, don't challenge the customer

You create such a climate by reinforcing customer behaviors, not by challenging them. The natural tendency is to react to complaints with some defensiveness. Instead, we should react with encouragement. An auto dealership service manager I know does a good job with this. I called to tell him of a funny noise coming from my car after it had just been serviced. Instead of asking me a bunch of questions about the kind of noise, or, worse yet, implying in some way that the noise may be my fault, he immediately said, "That's not good. We better get that fixed for you." I didn't have to explain, justify, or diagnose (although later he tactfully asked for some additional details about the nature of the noise). I told him of my complaint, and he immediately projected an attitude of "let's get this fixed for you."

## Be sensitive to your first reactions

The first comments out of your mouth when a customer begins to complain will largely determine the quality and quantity of feedback you will get. Like my auto-service guy, make those first comments positive and helpful.

Avoid acting defensively or making unnecessary demands for details. Accept the fact that the complaint is legitimate because it is real to the customer or upset employee. Don't justify, or even try to explain, your reaction until you hear the whole story.

In face-to-face situations, maintain eye contact and use nonverbal behaviors that show your interest in hearing it all. Be careful of facial expression (like a smirk, or look of boredom) that may discount the customer. If your contact is by phone, avoid dead air or prolonged silences, which may convey skepticism or disinterest.

Avoid any comments that would be construed as challenging the customer. If you suspect that the problem may be caused by customer misuse of the product, wait until the whole complaint is expressed and then ask some tactful questions about how the product was used. The issue is not whether the customer or the company is "right." The productive attitude is one of cooperation and problem solving.

## Try the Allegiance Technologies Active Listening System

Before I talk about how to best act on customer or employee complaints, I want to introduce you to a Web-based "active listening system" (ALS)[2] that provides an exceptional turn-key customer and employee dialoguing tool. After you read this, I encourage you to take a few moments to go to **www.AllegianceTech.com** and look at the system's demo.

Allegiance Technologies' approach differs from its competitors. Several other companies are building Web sites for collecting customer feedback (especially complaints). Customers can go to these sites to describe their experiences. However, the goal of some such budding sites is to encourage consumers to vent their wrath—then collate, cross-reference, and sell these complaints as marketing research. The intended buyers of this research are the same companies that are enduring public Web whippings.[3] The marketing-information-collection approach seems self-serving at best and, I believe, undercuts the company's credibility for resolving issues and building loyalty. It reflects a "what's-in-it-for-me" mentality rather than an honest attempt at building mutually valuable relationships.

Still other companies use standard surveys or other polling processes to gather data. While of some value, these data are typically provided at the request of the company rather than initiated by the customer or employee. Customer- or employee-initiated input is more genuine and reliable.

Allegiance Technologies' approach gathers four kinds of customer input: complaints, compliments, questions, and suggestions. This input is directed to the client company and is not publicly aired. The system also provides measures of customer allegiance and satisfaction before and after the company responds to the feedback. The person filing a complaint is also asked what he or she would like to see the company do to remedy the situation. In this way, the customer or employee is drawn into a dialogue and enjoys engagement with the company. The feeling of engagement goes a long way toward earning allegiance and building confidence in management.

Allegiance Technologies sells three versions of the ALS—one for customers, one for employees, and one for partners. All three versions follow the same general format. Client organizations subscribe to the hosted service, which is modestly priced—less expensive than the cost of developing a similar in-house system.

By having a neutral third party acting as a conduit between the customer (or employee) and the organization, frank and open communication can be achieved. Any feedback can be submitted anonymously; the person giving the feedback need only provide an email address to Allegiance, not to the client company. This anonymity feature makes the system especially useful for employees who may fear retaliation. (It can be useful for government-mandated processes for facilitating whistle blowing on company misdeeds.)

Customers or employees who do not have Web access can submit feedback by telephone, at kiosks, or in person. Designated representatives then enter the comments in the system.

Allegiance Technologies has maintained the enviable record of 100% customer retention. Since its founding in 2000, every customer has renewed its subscription. The company continues to add feedback-management capabilities and works with several consulting firms that provide client companies with specific direction for strategic and tactical application of customer-generated feedback. The active listening system has become an integral part of the way these organizations do business.

The following pages show some screen displays of the Allegiance Technologies system. The sample screens show an active listening system for a bank or financial institution. These are modified for other types of businesses, but these shots give you the general idea. To view other details, view the Allegiance Technologies website at **www.AllegianceTech.com**.

## Act on Complaints in Productive Ways

With systems such as Allegiance Technologies' ALS, companies accomplish the first important step—they show customers and employees that they are serious about receiving feedback and establishing a dialogue. The second step is to respond to feedback quickly and in constructive ways.

Timing is critical when you get customer or employee input. Early recovery is far easier than letting a bad situation fester and then trying to fix it. Act on complaints quickly, tactfully, and efficiently using a three-step process of (1) feeling empathy, (2) resolving the problem, and (3) offering something more to exceed what the customer anticipates.

## Input Customer Feedback

Regional Financial employees can use this page to enter feedback on behalf of customers. Feedback will be aggregated and automatically routed to the appropriate Regional Financial manager.

If you have questions or comments about this system, want to find out the status of an item you entered, or want to add additional comments to an item, please contact your manager.

**Feedback Classification**

Please select the type of feedback:

| Input a COMPLAINT ▼ |

Please select the feedback source:

| In-Person ▼ |

This feedback is about:
(you must select a location with a '>' in front of it)

```
Regional Financial
   Regional Financial Branch
      > Ogden Branch
      > Provo Branch
      > West Jordan Branch
      > ZCMI Center
   Regional Financial Department
      > Bank Card
      > Mortgage
      > Trusts
   > Regional Financial Overall
   > Regional Financial Online Banking
```

**Employee Information**
(Items marked with an (*) asterisk are required)

*Employee name (person entering this feedback):          Employee e-mail address:

| | | |

**Customer Information**
(Please provide as much information as you can. If feedback is from someone who is not a customer, please make note of it in the Feedback Information section.)

Account number:

First name:

Last name:

(if business account, input Last name/business name. ex: Smith / Acme Co.)

Phone:

E-mail address:

Customer requires additional follow-up: (If yes, please provide the appropriate contact information in the fields above.)
   ⊙ Yes   ○ No

Customer prefers future contact regarding this feedback via:
   ⊙ E-mail   ○ Phone   ○ Letter

**Feedback Information**

1. From the customer's perspective, what is the COMPLAINT regarding?

Please make a selection ▾

2. Please describe the COMPLAINT.
   (Information entered in this field MAY BE viewable by the customer.)

Spell Check

3. What would the customer like done to resolve this issue?
   (Information entered in this field MAY BE viewable by the customer.)

Spell Check

4. Is this feedback regarding a particular employee? (If yes, input employee name. If no, leave blank)

5. Estimate the date of service.

January ▾ 30 ▾ 2004 ▾

**Input Notes**

Enter the details of anything you did to resolve the issue, start the resolution process, or respond to the customer.

Resolution/Notes:
(Information entered in this field WILL NOT be viewable by the customer.)

Spell Check

Status:

Open ▾

[ Submit Feedback ]

Customers or employees use an input form such as this one at the Allegiance Technologies website to enter feedback, suggestions, complaints, and compliments about the client organization.

Efficiency of responses is easily monitored by the ALS. In both the customer and employee versions, a built-in clock provides metrics that indicate how long it takes to respond and close out a dialogue. Managers can quickly determine the status of any input and, if necessary, provide resources needed to make response times acceptable. Nothing impresses people as significantly as quick follow-up.

Below are some tips for responding once input is received.

## Feel the customer's pain

Recognize that upset customers are likely to be disappointed, angry, frustrated, or even in pain—and they blame you to some extent. Typically they want you to do some or all of the following:

- Treat them with respect and empathy
- Listen to their concerns, understand their problems, and take them seriously
- Compensate them or provide restitution for the unsatisfactory product or service
- Share their sense of urgency; get their problems handled quickly
- Avoid further inconvenience
- Punish someone for the problem (sometimes)
- Assure them the problem will not happen again.

Some employees have trouble knowing how to phrase their concern to an upset customer. One model for communicating in such situations is called the feel, felt, found approach. Seminar leader and author Rebecca Morgan teaches the feel, felt, found approach as a suggested way to express ideas so that upset customers won't become more upset.[4] This technique acknowledges the customer's feelings and offers an explanation in a way he or she can listen to. Morgan suggests using this kind of wording:

- "I understand how you could *feel* that way."
- "Others have *felt* that way too."
- "And then they *found*, after an explanation, that [this policy actually protects them, so it made sense (or some other suggestion)]."

The first two statements can be used verbatim. The third is an opportunity to explain what can or cannot be done to help solve the problem. Be careful to avoid saying "I know how you feel"—you can't know exactly how another person feels. Better wording is "I can understand how (or why) you'd feel that way."

## Do all you can to resolve the problem

An acceptable solution to a problem may be perceived differently by different people. One reason the Allegiance Technologies system is so effective is that it asks the complaining person what he or she would regard as an appropriate solution. Often, the complaining party requests something less drastic that the company would be willing to do. Do what is requested, and the problem is resolved.

## Go beyond by offering symbolic atonement

When attempting to recover an unhappy customer, the icing on the cake is the something extra you give to make up for the problem. Suppose you buy a new pair of shoes and the heel falls off. You call the shoe store and the owner says to bring them back and he'll replace them. You take time off from work, drive downtown to the store, battle for a parking space, and spend about an hour doing this. He cheerfully gives you a new pair of shoes. Are you satisfied now?

Probably not. Why? Because he really hasn't repaid you for your inconvenience. Sure, he stood behind the product and perhaps even did so in a pleasant manner, but you still came out on the short end.

What kinds of things can we do to reconcile this type of problem? Here are a few possible ideas that could be seen as going the extra mile in the eyes of a customer:

- *Offer to pick up or deliver* goods to be replaced or repaired. Auto dealerships win allegiance by offering to pick up the customer's car rather than having the customer bring it in when a recall notice requires something to be fixed.

- *Give a gift* of merchandise to repay for inconvenience. The gift may be small, but the thought will be appreciated. Things like a free dessert for the restaurant customer who endures slow service and extra copies of a print job to offset a minor delay are examples. It's the thought that counts.

- *Reimburse* for costs of returning merchandise, such as parking fees or shipping costs. (Mail-order retailers pay all return-postage fees to reduce customer annoyance and inconvenience.)

- *Acknowledge* the customer's inconvenience and thank him for giving you the opportunity to try to make it right. A sincere apology can go a long way. Make the wording of the apology sincere and personal. Say, "I'm sorry you had to wait," rather than, "The company regrets the delay." You express empathy with statements like, "I can imagine how aggravating it can be . . ." or "I hate when that happens, and I'm sorry you had to go through . . ."

- *Follow-up to see that the problem was handled.* Don't assume the customer's difficulty has been fixed unless you handled it yourself and have checked with the customer to see that the fix held up. (The Allegiance ALS polls customers and re-measures their satisfaction level to confirm that the complaint really has been resolved.)

You may not have the authority to do all of these things (although many cost little or nothing) but you can be the customer's advocate. If all goes well, you should feel a genuine sense of satisfaction after handling an unhappy or irate customer or employee.

## Keep emotion out of recovery

Often you can creatively recover an unhappy customer, but this is not a perfect world and people are not always rational. Sometimes the complainer gets to you and you get upset. Work to avoid letting anger or frustration reflect back on that customer or other customers. This can be difficult. To succeed, remember these key points:

- *Don't beat yourself up.* If you *try your best to satisfy* the customer, you have done all that you can do. No one can ask for more.

- *Don't take it personally.* Upset people often say things they don't really mean. They are blowing off steam, venting frustration. If the problem was really your fault, resolve to learn from the experience and do better next time. If you had no control over the situation, do what you can, but don't bat your head against the wall.

- *Don't rehash the experience* with your co-workers or in your own mind. What's done is done. Recounting the experience with others probably won't make their day any better, and rehashing it to yourself will just make you mad. You may, however, want to ask another person how they would have handled the situation.

## Look back and learn

When the customer situation has cooled, you may want to review how you handled the customer, with an eye toward improving your skills. Think back on the situation and ask questions like these:

- What triggered the customer's complaint? Was it primarily a value-, systems-, or people-generated problem?

- What would it take to fix such a problem? Is it possible to avoid?

- How did the customer see the problem? Who was to blame? What irritated him most? Why was he angry or frustrated?

- How did you see the problem? Was the customer partially to blame?
- What did you say to the customer that helped the situation?
- What did you say that seemed to aggravate the situation?
- How did you show your concern to the customer?
- What will you do differently if a similar complaint arises?

# Handling the Occasional Customer from Hell

"Stubbornness is the energy of fools," says the German proverb. Sometimes we need to draw the line between upset customers with legitimate problems and chronic complainers who consume our time with unreasonable demands—the dreaded "customer from hell." Here are some tips:

## Be sure this really is a chronic complainer

First, be certain you have got a *chronic* complainer. When you've tried the normal recovery approaches and nothing seems to work, look for the following telltale signs:[5]

- They always seem to look for someone to blame. In their world, there is no such thing as an accident: Someone is always at fault, and it's probably you.

- They never admit any degree of fault or responsibility. They see themselves as blameless and victims of the incompetence or malice of others.

- They have strong ideas about what others should do. They love to define other peoples' duties. If you hear a complaint phrased exclusively in terms of what other people *always, never, must,* or *must not* do, chances are you're talking to a chronic complainer.

- They complain at length. While normal complainers pause for breath every now and then, chronics seem able to inhale while saying the words, "and another thing . . ."

## What to do with this guy (or gal)

When faced with that occasional chronic complainer (they really are quite rare, fortunately), try these techniques:

- Actively listen to identify the legitimate grievance beneath the endless griping.

- Rephrase the complainer's main points in your own words, even if you have to interrupt to do so. Say something like, "Excuse me, but do I understand you to say that the service wasn't finished on time and you feel frustrated and annoyed?"

- Establish the *facts* to reduce the complainer's tendency to exaggerate or over-generalize. If he says he "tried calling all day but as usual you tried to avoid me," tactfully establish the actual number of times called and when.

- Resist the temptation to apologize, although that may seem to be the natural thing to do. Since the main thing the complainer is trying to do is fix blame—not solve problems—your apology will be seen as an open invitation to further blaming. Instead, ask questions like, "Would an extended warranty solve your problem?" or "When would be the best time for me to call you back with that information?"

- Force the complainer to pose solutions to the problem, especially if he doesn't seem to like your ideas. Also, try putting a time limit on the conversation by saying something like, "I have to talk with someone in 10 minutes. What sort of action plan can we work out in that time?" The object of this approach is to get him away from whining and into a problem-solving mode.

We have, of course, no guarantees when dealing with such customers, but the effort may well be worth it. Converting one of these folks into a normal, rational customer can be professionally rewarding. If it doesn't work, so be it. You've given your best, and that's all anyone can ask.

## Maintain a Feedback Log

Feedback can be valuable and should be captured. As a minimum, create a complaint log. The shortest pencil is better than the longest memory. So get in the habit of jotting down descriptions of complaints received and actions taken to resolve them. Use the complaint log as a part of regular staff meetings, where you can discuss how the situation has been handled or brainstorm other ways it could be done.

The Allegiance Technologies Active Listening System captures and records all customer and employee dialogues. This captured information can be invaluable when addressing value, systems, and people turnoffs. The dialogue provides a clear description of who said what to whom and when the comments were made. The ALS also has an escalation feature, showing how complaints are passed up to people with the authority to deal with the problems. All this data allows precise analysis of any dialogue with customers and employees. The ALS website screen on the next page shows the Allegiance Technologies' response detail. It accurately tracks all interaction with the customer or employee.

## One More Time—Be Open to Feedback

The central theme of this chapter is that a critical ingredient in improving experiences for your company's customers and employees is your receptiveness to feedback—even from your most severe critics. This, of course, can be painful. But it can also be exceptionally valuable.

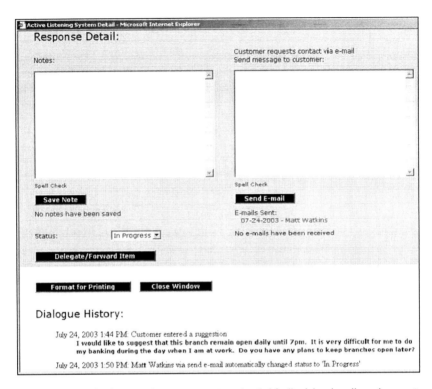

The Allegiance Technologies ALS system maintains a detailed feedback log that allows the organization to more effectively address value, systems, and people turnoffs.

## Feedback receptiveness is an attitude

Less-successful business people prefer to be ostriches. They bury their heads and tune out all negative comments. They reward other people in their organization for *not* receiving any complaints. In doing so, they never learn what they need to know to improve. But remember, the ostrich always leaves one end exposed.

For most people, giving criticism (even in a constructive way) is risky. When customers first offer such feedback, they watch closely to gauge the response. The reaction they receive will usually determine whether they will offer feedback again.

Think back to the last time you received criticism from someone else. To what degree did you employ the following tips for encouraging continuing feedback?

## Some tips for encouraging continuous feedback:

- **Avoid being defensive.** Listen—don't explain or justify. Learn to withhold your response. While someone criticizes you is not the time to explain or justify your actions, even if you feel the criticism is unwarranted or stems from a misunderstanding. Listen now, explain later. Your being defensive stifles feedback. It tells others you are more interested in justifying yourself than in understanding what they are saying.

- **Ask for more information,** especially for specifics. This is a good opportunity to obtain more information. Honest questions will support and encourage the continued flow of feedback. For example, say, "That's very helpful. Tell me more. Is there anything else I should know about that?"

- **Express an honest reaction.** You certainly have a right to express your feelings about the feedback received. You may well say, "I'm a little surprised (or frustrated or disappointed) you had that experience, but you may have a point," or "I'm not sure what to say. I never even thought of that, but I will from now on."

- **Thank the people providing feedback.** Let them know that you realize how risky giving feedback can be, and express your appreciation for their efforts.

Using these kinds of communication behaviors gives you the opportunity to avoid turning off future feedback that could be valuable to you.

In all honesty, many people find it difficult to use these tips. In most cases, their ego gets in the way. They feel they are being diminished in some way by not "fighting back." But that is precisely the point. These situations should not be seen as conflicts but as mutually beneficial problem-solving opportunities.

It takes a lot of courage to seek out and really hear feedback—especially criticism. But the successful businessperson is willing to do what the oblivious ostrich is not. The payoff for success in earning the allegiance of customers and employees is enormous.

## Notes

1. These Office of Consumer Affairs statistics are quoted in *The Customer Service Manager's Handbook of People Power Strategies* (Englewood Cliffs, NJ: Prentice-Hall, Inc., 1999), p. 3.

2. Allegiance Technologies is a professional-services firm specializing in helping organizations build customer and employee allegiance using its "Active Listening System." For further information, see the company's Website at **www.AllegianceTech.com**.

3. Thomas E. Weber, "Can Your Complaints, Adroitly Repackaged, Build a Web Business?" *Wall Street Journal*, January 10, 2000, p. B1.

4. R. L. Morgan, *Calming Upset Customers* (Menlo Park, CA: Crisp Publications, 1989), p. 40.

5. Adapted from "How to Deal With Those Chronic Complainers," in *Customer Service Manager's Letter*, September 20, 1989. Published by Prentice-Hall Professional Newsletters. The article is based on the work of Dr. Robert Bramson, *Coping with Difficult People* (New York: Dell, 1988).

# Chapter 4

# Creating a Positive Imbalance with Customers and Employees

A s a rule, people can get used to anything. If the chances of winning the lottery are a gazillion to one, they don't expect to win—they hope to win. But if their overnight package doesn't arrive, they are seriously aggravated. If the milk they just bought at the store is sour, they're up in arms. If you lead them to believe that they can expect full-on, full-time, no-holds-barred customer service on your Web site—and they can't—you will have made an enemy where you could have made a friend.[1]

—Jim Sterne, *Customer Service in the Internet*

## The Way It Is . . .

A participant at one of my training sessions told me this story: "I have a younger sister who is nine years younger than I. When I left home at 18, she was still a little girl. She grew up and married a fellow named Travis. They lived a thousand miles from me. I barely knew Travis. We got together at family parties once every year or two, and I chatted with him for a few moments when I'd call my sister. But our relationship was nothing more than that.

"One day I was in a book store and I saw the paperback of Tom Clancy's first book, *The Hunt for Red October*. Well, Travis had been in the nuclear Navy and I thought he might enjoy this book. So I sprang for the five bucks and got a copy, wrote a little note in it, and sent it to Travis. It wasn't his birthday; it wasn't Christmas. I just felt like sending him a book I thought he'd enjoy.

"Well, he was blown over by this. He couldn't believe that someone would do that, and he called me immediately and we had a long chat. A few months later, he sent me a videotape on how to improve my golf game.

"The outcome of this was that we have become quite close. The whole relationship changed because of a simple unexpected gift."

## The Role of Balance in Relationships

Human beings are social creatures, constantly going into and out of relationships with others. Some relationships are long lasting, such as family and lifelong friends. Some relationships are fleeting. They may last for only a few minutes, such as a brief transaction at a service station while traveling cross-country. You may say hello and perhaps chat about the weather, but then you never see that person again.

Social psychology teaches that all relationships have a need to establish a balance, a sense of fairness. What we give to the relationship must balance in some way with what we get from it. If we feel that we give far more than we receive (or vice versa), we are likely to feel some psychological discomfort.

Simple examples of such discomfort might arise when we say hello to someone and they look right at us but ignore our greeting. Or imagine that in a social situation you invite someone to your home for dinner. After dinner, your guest leaves and never even says thank you. You'd certainly feel some psychological discomfort, perhaps wondering what was wrong with that person—or what was wrong with you.

Knowledge of this psychological phenomenon is useful as we consider the tactic in this chapter: creating positive imbalance with customers. I'll explain why in a moment. First, let's consider why customers act as they do.

At a basic psychological level, people are motivated to act in a particular way because their action will either result in a gain (reward) or avoid a loss (punishment). Customers and employees are rational people. If a buying experience or a job activity is positive, they will see it as a gain and probably come back; if the experience is negative, they'll regard it as a loss and try to avoid returning. If it's so-so, they'll stay in a zone of indifference, being neither motivated nor de-motivated.

## The Customer's "Zone of Indifference"

The correlation between customer satisfaction and allegiance to an organization can be rather tenuous. Even satisfied customers and employees may be neutral in their relationship with a business. Some little thing can push them over the edge toward dissatisfaction. Service or employee-relations efforts can meet their needs adequately but fail to earn their continuing allegiance. Motivation researcher Friedrick Herzberg[2] and others discovered long ago that satisfied workers are not necessarily motivated workers. Likewise, satisfied customers cannot be assumed to be motivated repeat customers. A "zone of indifference" exists between the satisfied and the motivated. In this zone, things are okay, but there is little to tie the customer to the company in the long run. Herzberg argues that satisfaction and motivation are on two different continuums. The factors that *motivate* people are different from the factors that simply *prevent dissatisfaction*.

Actually, customers who are satisfied may be *inert*, not motivated. Their satisfaction simply means the *absence of dissatisfaction*, not the motivation to become a repeat customer. A zone of indifference lies between the dissatisfied and the motivated.

The Satisfaction-Motivation Distinction

The challenge for businesses is to get beyond customer and employee satisfaction to *motivation*. This is best done by responding to what people perceive as they compare reality with what was anticipated. Incongruent expectations lie at the root of all conflict.

# The Crucial Role of Customer Anticipation

Customers entering into a transaction anticipate (albeit perhaps unconsciously) a certain kind of experience; they expect to be treated a particular way. What they anticipate is often based on their past associations with this business, person, or organization, or with ones they see as similar. If the customer had a good experience in the past, he or she will probably anticipate something satisfactory. If the last transaction wasn't positive, the customer might assume the next one won't be any better.

What customers anticipate is *perceptual*. It exists in the customer's mind. Sometimes these perceptions are accurate and rational; sometimes they aren't. And to make matters even more challenging for service providers, perceptions are ever-changing, presenting a moving, hard-to-define target.

## Anticipating the core product or service

When people judge the quality of a tangible product, they use fairly objective and somewhat predictable standards. For example, when people buy a new automobile, they'll be likely to judge its quality by things like

- driving and handling characteristics

- low frequency of repair (it seldom has to be fixed)

- appropriate size (it holds my family comfortably)

- a good price relative to its quality

- workmanship (it seems to be well built and has a nice paint job).

Likewise, when judging the quality of a service (say, a house painter's job), people will measure it by such standards as

- whether the work was done on time (the painter met the deadline)

- whether the surfaces to be painted were carefully prepared

- whether the paints were mixed and applied neatly

- whether the painter cleaned up after the job.

These kinds of standards are relatively predictable; they are much the same for each customer.

But evaluating the degree of customer satisfaction goes beyond the core product or service bought. It involves the entire buying *experience*. The standards by which customers measure overall satisfaction are more ambiguous.

(Although I am using customer examples here, employees, as an organization's internal customers, also face the same expectations. They expect, for example, that the benefits office will give clear information and that their supervisor will meet certain expectations, such as fairness, openness to ideas, accuracy of performance reviews, and so on.)

## Anticipating the whole buying experience

What customers anticipate about the core product is only part of the mental process they go through. People will anticipate different experiences with different organizations or under differing circumstances. They could buy the same core product from several places. They are, however, likely to anticipate different treatment from a "high-touch," full-service retailer than they do from a warehouse store. They would anticipate different service from a prestigious law firm than from a state auto-license bureau. They might well anticipate different experiences from a well-known technology firm's sales representative than they would from a catalogue distributor's Web site.

For that matter, people often anticipate something different from the same organization at different times. Perhaps they expect a little less personal attention during busy periods (like the Christmas season or end-of-month license plate deadline times).

## Different anticipations from different businesses

Suppose you intend to shop at a low-cost, self-service discount store, like a K-Mart, Target, or Fred Meyer. Going into the store, you anticipate being treated in a particular way. You do not necessarily expect the clerk in the clothing department (if you can find one) to be an expert in fitting clothing or to be particularly helpful in color coordinating items. This is not to say that some people who work there would not have these skills, but you probably wouldn't expect such skills, as a general rule.

If you simply select some clothing items and take them to a check-out for purchase, you are not surprised or disappointed—you expected unassisted self-service. The experience is what you anticipated and, if other aspects of the store are okay (it seems clean and well-stocked, for instance), you could be perfectly satisfied.

By contrast, if you go to a Nordstrom's, Macy's, or Bloomingdale's full-service department store or to an exclusive boutique, you will probably anticipate a different kind of transaction. You will probably expect sales people to have considerable expertise in clothing fit, color, and materials. You will realistically anticipate that clerks will give you full attention and assistance as you make your purchases.

When you experience situations like these just described, what you anticipate is validated—you get about what you expected. Dissatisfaction is probably avoided; you are likely to be in the zone of indifference.

## Using what customers anticipate to build allegiance

Getting customers beyond the zone of indifference is the goal. The key to motivating a customer to feel allegiance toward you, however, lies not in *meeting* what the customer anticipates but in *exceeding* it. To do this, you need to have some conception of what the customer anticipates.

How can you best anticipate changing customer needs? I think you already know this. Nothing is more important than staying close to your customers and employees by maintaining an ongoing dialogue. To do so requires every company member to be a sensing device, a curious information gatherer.

Three things are necessary for ongoing customer sensing:

• Employees who are taught to get, and are rewarded for getting, customer feedback.

• Processes for harvesting and using customer feedback.

- Empowered employees who respond to customer feedback in productive ways.

Customer perceptions are exceptionally valuable data. I talked in Chapter 3 about the critical importance of dialoguing with your customers and employees and recommended as one important tool the Allegiance Technologies' Active Listening System. ALS can provide an ongoing flow of information that teaches the company about customer wants, needs, and expectations. Only when we have a sense of what is wanted and anticipated can our organizations exceed expectations and thus earn customer allegiance. Ultimately, today's customer-service and employee-relations successes arise from a central theme, an underlying principle, that is simple to state yet challenging to implement. The underlying principle is—

*You achieve customer and employee satisfaction, retention, and allegiance by exceeding what people anticipate in positive ways.*

The rest of this book builds on this critical theme and provides specific tactics for applying this principle.

# The Concept of A-Plus

I call this process of exceeding the anticipated *A-Plus*[†]. Research and the experience of countless experts points to A-Plus as almost a "master key" to service success. In the following discussions, I again focus on customers, but every principle also applies to an organization's internal customers—the employees.

As customers compare what they anticipate with the service received, one of three situations will show up:

---

[†]I used to call this "E-Plus," playing on the word *expectations,* but found that the letter E has been working overtime with references to electronic matter (email, e-commerce, e-business, etc.).

**Situation 1:** The experience was not as positive (or was more negative) than the customer anticipated.

**Situation 2:** The experience was pretty much what the customer anticipated.

**Situation 3:** The experience was more positive (or less negative) than the customer anticipated.

In the condition described in Situation 1, the customer's experience was not very good. She's dissatisfied and likely to defect to another provider, if she has a rational alternative.

In the condition described in Situation 2, the customer is neither dissatisfied nor particularly motivated to return. This is the zone of indifference we discussed earlier.

In Situation 3, the transaction was better than anticipated. Either the customer thought it would be pretty good and it was very good, or the customer thought it would not be particularly good but it wasn't as bad as anticipated. If positive expectations were sufficiently exceeded (or negative ones shown to be unfounded), this customer is a very good candidate for repeat business.

Situation 3 is what I call an *A-Plus* experience—customer anticipations were *exceeded* in positive ways.

# How A-Plus Builds Customer and Employee Allegiance

A concept from the field of social psychology called *equity theory* provides a solid theoretical basis for predicting that the customer who experiences A-Plus service is more likely to become a repeat customer. Psychologist J. Stacy Adams first articulated this theory in the mid-1960s. It has stood the test of time to be widely accepted as a predictor of human behavior. Here is a quick summary of the theory:

## A brief description of equity theory

Equity theory starts with the premise I described earlier—that human beings constantly go into and out of various kinds of relationships ranging from the intimate to the cursory. The buyer-seller or employer-employee relationships are germane to this discussion.

Once in a relationship, even a brief one, people regularly assess the *relative equity or fairness of their involvement* compared to other people in the relationship. They check to see if what they give to the relationship seems appropriate for what they are getting out of it. A very simple example of a relationship that is out of balance (inequitable) would arise if you gave something (a tangible gift, a greeting, a special favor) and received nothing in return.

Inequitable relationships feel awkward and often uncomfortable. Common courtesy demands that we do something to rebalance the relationship. When invited to dinner, people strive to rebalance by bringing something to share at the meal, or a hostess gift, or the like. Or the guest invites the hostess to something. This re-balancing is ingrained in social mores of most cultures. People who take but never give are soon found lonely.

Much of the early testing of this theory focused on the workplace, where workers' perceptions of fairness (equity) were correlated with certain behaviors. Not surprisingly, studies found that people who were paid less for doing the same work as others, for example, felt a sense of inequity. In my own doctoral dissertation, I found that employees who sensed that their supervisor communicated more often and more positively with other employees in the workgroup felt a clear sense of inequity.[3]

The theory goes beyond simply citing situations where people may feel inequitably treated. It also predicts what people are likely to do about this feeling. When inequity is perceived, people will respond with one of the following reactions or with some combination of them:

- *Ignore or rationalize the inequity.* (The offended person makes up a reason. "He deserves to be treated better than I," "The world isn't fair, but I'm not going to fight it," or "I guess he didn't hear me say hello.")

- *Demand restitution.* (The offended employee goes to the boss to demand fairer pay, or the customer wants her money back when product quality is poor.)

- *Retaliate.* (The offended person tells others about how bad the organization is, does harm to the person seen as the cause of the inequity, or engages in outright sabotage.)

- *Withdraw from the relationship.* (The offended person quits the relationship and doesn't come back.)

So far, this theory seems to bear out common sense. If we feel we are being unfairly treated, we get upset and usually do something about it. Hence, the unsatisfied participant in a relationship (the customer or employee, in our case) is likely to do one of these things. The first two alternatives may give you a chance to patch things up and retain the customer using recovery techniques such as those learned in Chapter 3. But the last two—retaliation or withdrawal—can be devastating. Mrs. Williams, the former Happy Jack's Super Market customer in our Chapter 2 story, did both. She withdrew—quit shopping there—and retaliated by telling her friends, thus starting the negative ripple effects that may have resulted in scores or even hundreds of lost customers or potential customers.

## The positive side of equity theory

Here is where the theory gets even more interesting: *People who feel that they are receiving more than they "deserve" from a transaction also experience a psychological need to restore the balance of fairness.* A simple illustration of this is the psychological pressure you may feel to reciprocate when someone does something unusually nice for you. The relationship will remain unbalanced until you rebalance it with a similar kindness or some other positive action.

Herein lies the theoretical basis for our A-Plus strategy for exceeding customer and employee expectations. By going beyond what people anticipate, you create an imbalance that, for many people, will be a catalyst for action on their part to rebalance. The logical options are the opposite of what the victims of negative imbalance feel: They could rationalize or ignore it, of course, but attempts to restore the balance could also take the form of telling others of the positive experience, paying a premium for the goods received, or, in short, becoming a loyal customer.

The challenge, then, is to *create positive imbalances by exceeding what customers and employees anticipate.* This is the master key to creating an A-Plus strategy for earning the allegiance of customers and employees.

## Putting the A-Plus Strategy to Work

Putting the A-Plus strategy to work requires two kinds of ongoing actions:

1. Continually work to understand what customers and employees anticipate, and then

2. Exceed what customers and employees anticipate.

Companies have (in addition to the Active Listening System described earlier) several ways to get a sharper picture of what customers and employees are anticipating:

• fishing for feedback,

• focus groups, and

• explorer groups.

Lets' look at each of these.

## Fish for feedback with naive listening

The best way to fish for feedback as an everyday activity is with *naïve* listening. Naive listening is more of an attitude than a strategy. As its name implies, this kind of listening conveys that you don't know—are naive—about what customers want. Your task is to get them to explain it to you. Create an atmosphere where you and your people are cheerfully receptive to customer comments, even—*especially*—comments that might not be pleasant to hear. Then provide multiple channels for them to tell you what's on their minds. In prompting customers to share what they're thinking, use open-ended questions to get the most information.

Open-ended questions cannot be answered with a simple yes, no, or other simple response but instead encourage a considered, meaningful response. For example, restaurant servers who ask an open-ended question like, "How else can I make your dinner enjoyable?" will get a broader range of responses than one who asks the more common, "Do you need anything else?" ("No.") or "Is everything okay?" ("Yes.").

## Use focus groups

Focus groups have long been used for marketing research, and they can play an important role in understanding customer and employee perceptions and expectations as well. Although some marketing consultants may disagree with me, there's no great mystery to how focus groups work, and any intelligent person could run one effectively.

Here is the procedure for creating and getting the most from a focus group:

- Select a sample of your customers or employees to join with you in the focus-group session. Don't pick just people you know or customers you like. You may, however, want to be sure they are among your better customers by qualifying them according to their influence or how much they spend with you.

- Formally invite the customers or employees to participate, telling them when and where the focus group will meet, as well as how long the session will take. Let them know the reason: that you are attempting to better understand their needs and how you can better be of service to them.

- Limit your focus group to not fewer than five or more than a dozen people. Ask customers to confirm their attendance, but expect that some will not show up. Fifteen confirmed reservations will generally get you twelve actual participants. Follow up with phone calls to confirm attendance.

- Reward focus-group participants. Tell those invited that you will give them something for their participation. Retail stores may give focus-group participants a gift certificate, a free dinner, or even cash. In marketing research, it's not uncommon to pay people $50 or more for a one- or two-hour session.

When running the focus groups:

- Set the stage by having someone from top management moderate the group.

- Create an open atmosphere where participants will feel comfortable giving you all kinds of feedback. Be polite, open, encouraging, and receptive.

- Avoid cutting people off when they're making a critical comment, and do not, above all, be defensive of the way you're doing things now, when in the eyes of the customer it's not working.

- Keep any follow-up questions open-ended. Don't interrogate.

- Acknowledge compliments that group members may express, and thank the contributors for the compliments. Then make a statement such as, "We're happy to hear that we are doing things you like. Our major purpose here is to identify ways we can do a better job in meeting your needs. How can we do even better?"

- Limit the group to a predetermined amount of time; typically a one-hour or 90-minute (maximum) session works best. Focus-group sessions that are any longer than that will start to lose people's interest.

- Tape record the entire focus-group session and transcribe key notes for review. As you analyze the results of the group session, look for key words that might tip you off to what customers are looking for.

- At the end of the focus-group session, of course, be sure to thank the participants for all of their input—and give them their pay.

The critical key to successful focus groups is careful analysis of the information you receive. It is almost always necessary to transcribe, word-for-word, the entire discussion and to read this transcription carefully—several times. This transcript review can be laborious, but the careful processing of the raw data can lead to important insights about customer and employee perceptions that might never come out in other feedback sessions.

## Use explorer groups

Explorer groups go to other businesses to see how they do things. When you hear about a great idea another business is using, send out an explorer group to scope it out. One retailer known for exceptional service encourages employees to take a company van and rush to the scene of a great service idea used by other companies. They take notes and discuss possible implementation in their store. Explorer groups need not be sent only to direct competitors; often totally unrelated businesses have great ideas you can use.

Another way to gather great data is to "explore" how your own organization is serving customers by being a "customer." Call the company and listen to the impression created by the person answering the phone. Is this what your customer is hearing? How do you like it? Then visit other locations or areas in your own organization and see how you are treated.

Go fishing for feedback—regularly. Use ongoing naive listening, focus groups, and explorer groups to assess your business and your competition through the eyes of your customers. Open the communication channels, and give your customers opportunities to comment and complain using a proven process, such as the Allegiance Technologies ALS.

Remember, the vast majority of unhappy customers who do not complain will defect to another source of products or services. Of those who do complain and *have their problems addressed (even if not fully resolved)*, only five percent will abandon your business. In a sense, your complaining customers are your best customers. Meeting their needs provides an opportunity to solidify a business relationship and earn their allegiance.

As I said earlier, putting the A-Plus strategy to work requires two kinds of ongoing actions. The first, continually working to understand what customers and employees anticipate, is accomplished with multiple techniques to gather ongoing information. The second action, continually adjusting to exceed what customers and employees anticipate, is the focus of the remainder of this book. In the following chapters, I will show you a series of powerful ways to apply an A-plus strategy for earning customer and employee allegiance.

## Notes

1. Jim Sterne, *Customer Service in the Internet,* (New York: John Wiley & Sons, 1996), p. 46.

2. F. Herzberg, B. Mausner, and B. Snyderman, *The Motivation to Work*, 2nd ed. (New York: Wiley, 1959).

3. Paul R. Timm, "Effects of Inequity in Supervisory Communication Behavior on Subordinates in Clerical Workgroups," Florida State University, 1977. Unpublished doctoral dissertation.

# Chapter 5

# Giving A-Plus Value

> Unless companies want to be in a commoditized business, they will be compelled to upgrade their offerings to the next stage of economic value.
>
> —B. Joseph Pine and James H. Gilmore[1]

## The Way It Is . . .

You can find exceptional value in some unusual places. A recent *Wall Street Journal* article sang the praises of the public toilets in Suwon, South Korea. The city is so proud of its exceptional toilet facilities that it gives weekly tours to show them off to tourists. The public restroom is inside a building with the sloping wooden roof of a traditional Korean pavilion. Guests are invited to try out its heated toilet seats, examine the sinks, and take pictures . . . Violin music plays in the background, and small paintings of the Korean countryside hang on the walls . . . The facilities have bouquets of flowers (both fake and genuine), automatic faucets, sliding stall doors for the disabled, and solar-powered heat. Speakers pipe in Vivaldi's "Four Seasons," Korean palace music, or recordings of chirping birds."[2]

The perception of value is highly subjective, but people seem to know value when they experience it. While long-term durability or utility is often seen as the ultimate value, companies generally cannot wait the many years needed for their customers to recognize that long-term value. What companies can do is focus on creating an enhanced *sense* or *perception* of customer value, just as the city of Suwon did with its exceptional toilet facilities.

## A-Plus Value: What It Is

I talked in Chapter 2 about poor value as one of the three categories of customer turnoffs. In this chapter, we will consider *perceptions of value* as one way to create an A-Plus, allegiance-building experience. We can build customer allegiance by giving customers an enhanced *perception* of value—something that exceeds what they anticipate. But what, exactly, is perception of value?

Perception of value is a person's sense of a product's *quality* relative to its *cost*. For example, if you purchased a cheap throw-away product, say, an inexpensive disposable camera that cost less than $10, and the picture quality was not quite up to studio quality, you probably would not be overly upset. The camera's quality, relative to its cost, is what you anticipated—you expected snapshots, not professional portraits. If, however, you spent $900 for a deluxe camera with many professional features, you would have high expectations for the quality of the pictures the camera would produce. If the pictures were no better than those produced by a cheap camera, you'd have a right to be upset. You would have a *diminished* perception of the camera's value.

Likewise, if you gave a kid a few dollars to mow your lawn and he didn't get it exactly right, you'd chalk it up to a learning experience. Your perception of value would be satisfactory—you got what you paid for, and probably what you expected. But if you hired an expensive lawn-care professional and the work wasn't up to snuff, your perception of value would likely be reduced or diminished because you didn't get what you expected, considering what you paid. You expect to get what you pay for; and the more you pay, the more you expect.

# The Cost of Diminished Perceptions of Value

Sometimes even good companies let their quality slip, and customers eventually catch on to the quality deficit. And a company's failure to perceive and then respond to customers' diminished perceptions of value (the opposite of A-Plus) can destroy a company.

In the 1980s and early 1990s, Volkswagen Corporation of America saw its sales drop by 90% from its 1970 high of over half a million cars to less than 50,000 in 1993. What happened?

Much of VW's competitive advantage in subcompact cars evaporated when competitors (especially the Japanese manufacturers) engaged in extended conversations with their customers and used feedback received to develop appealing features. While VW engineers knew the *"right"* way to position a steering wheel, Japanese compacts offered adjustable tilt wheels. While VW was certain that its radios were "just fine," competitors responded to customer desires for multi-speaker stereo sound. Little automotive details like cup holders and power locks—features not really central to the core product of reliable transportation—provided a competitive advantage to companies that listened to their customers.

VW didn't listen to its customers nearly enough. As a result, customers began to perceive VW as offering less value. By the early 90s, Volkswagen of America was fighting for its life. Fortunately, VW learned from this experience and has produced a remarkable turnaround. By the late 1990s, the company had regained its traditional position as one of the most innovative and successful auto manufacturers, and the company is now thriving. But it almost didn't make it after having paid a terrible price for not perceiving and responding to its customers' diminished perception of value.

## Understanding Perceptions of Value

Perception of value is based on individual views of intrinsic and extrinsic (or associated) factors. Understanding these factors is the starting point for creating A-Plus value experiences for your customers.

### Intrinsic value of the product itself

Intrinsic value of a product may not become evident for a long time. You don't fully appreciate the value until the truck has a hundred-thousand miles on it, or the legal document your attorney prepared holds up in court, or the house painting job still looks great years later. A recent story talks about diminished intrinsic value in hotel rooms: "Hotel room scrunch!" cries a *Wall Street Journal* (January 21, 2000) story on 16 hotels that are actively building smaller and smaller rooms while still charging premium rates. The smallest rooms were found at the Paramount in New York. It had only 101 square feet! Some hotels were offering as much as 75 percent off the price of their rooms in the under-225-square-foot range.

In my training sessions, I ask participants to talk about products or services that have exceeded their expectations in terms of intrinsic value. People often respond by mentioning unusually reliable products like Toyota automobiles and trucks,[3] Kirby vacuum cleaners, certain appliances, Craftsman tools, and the like. We can all think of products we have owned that have lasted a long time and earned our brand allegiance.

Value takes on another look for intangible products or services. With these products, accuracy and attention to detail of the product provider may be the hallmark of value. A utility, cable provider, or financial institution that gives customers consistently accurate, easy-to-read statements may be giving A-Plus service. The company that makes it easy for customers to contact it and then responds quickly to fix any errors or problems will be perceived by customers as high in value.

The opposite creates immediate and often lasting negative perceptions of value. The massive electrical blackout of August 2003 left almost a third of the U.S. in the dark and some 40 million people endangered by unreliable electric utilities. In a more localized example, the phones stopped working at the national reservation center of LOT Polish Airlines in New York a few years ago. The airline called the phone company's problem line at 9 a.m. Eleven hours later, after the reservations center had closed for the day, repair technicians arrived. Before all was fixed, the center was without phone service for 33 hours (*Wall Street Journal*, January 19, 2000). Without phones, LOT was essentially out of business, and an eleven-hour response time was, needless to say, inexcusable. The intrinsic value was clearly lacking.

Of the credit cards I carry, my favorites are the American Express Card and Discover Private Issue. I perceive higher intrinsic value in these products for two reasons: they give me airline miles or cash back, and when I need to call either of these I can speak to a live person almost immediately. Other cards linger in my wallet because, when I have a problem, they force me through a maze of telephone switching that is annoying and time-consuming. This live-person contact enhances my perception of intrinsic value.

Still another example of intrinsic value is the personal touch provided by some banks to their key clients (whether individuals or corporations). Each client is assigned a bank executive who is willing to meet personally with the client to oversee his or her financial needs. The status of having a personal banker is premium value for many people.

## Extrinsic or associated value

Extrinsic (or "associated") value goes beyond the core product. It is associated with the product, but it is not essential to it. Associated value involves more than whether an automobile starts and runs reliably or the degree to which an Internet service provider stays up and running. It encompasses the entire customer relationship.

Remember that value is *perceptual.* Since perception, by definition, is different for different individuals, some people may be turned on by a company's extrinsic value efforts while others may regard them as nothing more than what is expected, or, worse, as fluff.

Companies need to create conditions that improve the likelihood of customers seeing extrinsic or associated value favorably.

# How to Create an Enhanced Sense of Value

Some ways companies seek to enhance customers' perceptions of extrinsic or associated value include—

- Packaging
- Guarantees and warranties
- Goodness of product fit
- Memorability of product experience
- Uniqueness and shared values
- Company credibility
- Add-ons

Let's look at examples of each of these value enhancers.

## Build A-Plus value with packaging

Imagine going to a hardware store to buy a power drill. There you find a stack of the particular model you want. All but one of these is in its original package. What is the likelihood that you would select the one without a box? Zero, right? You will undoubtedly buy one in a box even knowing that you'll throw the box away when you get home. The box—the package—enhances the perception of value.

A business associate of mine occasionally gives me books he thinks will be useful in my consulting and training work. Sometimes, he simply hands me a copy of a recommended book. On a few occasions, he enhanced the value of his gift by writing a friendly note in the book and gift wrapping it.

The product is the same, but the gift-wrapped packaging and personalization enhance its perceived value. This illustrates the "little things" principle. Tiny differences make the extrinsic value of the product greater. While doing consulting work in Iceland, I shopped for some Icelandic wool gifts for my daughters. After receiving adequate but nondescript service in several shops, I found one store in Reykjavik called Vik Wool that had particularly friendly employees and a nice selection of knitted gloves. I selected two pairs and a few other small items. When the clerk rang up my goods, she wrapped each gift in a small, hand-knit sack tied with a ribbon. The little sacks were made of knitting remnants from their factory. The packaging of these inexpensive gifts far exceeded what I had anticipated. Other stores set the expectation with generic plastic bags; Vik Wool A-Pluses customers with the beautiful knitted wool sacks.

If your business sells intangibles, don't overlook possible packaging. If anything, packaging enhancements can be even more powerful when they are completely unexpected. But how do we package an intangible? Here are a few examples:

A successful insurance sales representative I know gives his clients their policies in an attractive leather portfolio, which can be used to store other important papers. He goes a step further by engraving the client's name on the portfolio. To this day, I have such a leather binder given to me almost 20 years ago. The extrinsic value of his product lives on.

If your customers receive only documents in exchange for their money (often the only tangible product associated with a service), give some thought to packaging these papers in an attractive or useful manner. Or add some tangible items that might relate to your services. AirTouch Cellular sent its best customers a road-travel gift set. It included a thermos, Starbucks coffee, and some snacks.

Upscale department stores have long known the value of attractive gift wrapping. Customers love it—especially customers like me who are all thumbs when it comes to wrapping gifts. But any organization can enhance its packaging and thus increase the customer's perception of value.

## Build A-Plus value with guarantees or warranties

Would you be likely to see a product with a lifetime warranty as having higher value than a similar product with a only a 30-day warranty? Most people do. I used to tell customers who purchased my videotape training programs that these were unconditionally guaranteed for 30 days. If they felt the programs did not meet their needs, they could return the videos within 30 days and get a full refund. Then I began to think about enhancing this sense of value and changed that guarantee to forever. If the customer ever felt the product did not meet his or her needs, it could be returned for a full refund.

I found that, with the unlimited guarantee period, the percent of goods returned was unchanged. In fact, with the 30-day guarantee, I may have actually been encouraging refund requests by setting a target date. The customer who had the product for 25 days or so may have felt some urgency to make a decision—and sometimes that decision was to send the product back. A lifetime guarantee eliminates the motivation to act now, thus reducing the likelihood the customer will return the product.

If your product has good intrinsic value, the return rates for short-term guarantees versus long-term or lifetime guarantees will be virtually equal.

Nordstrom's department stores have earned a tremendous amount of good publicity from their no-questions-asked, unconditional return policy. The oft-repeated story of the fellow who returned a set of tires to Nordstrom's (a store that doesn't sell tires!) has had incredible positive ripple effects. The tale has become legend and, when written about in Tom Peters and Robert Waterman's 1982 best seller, *In Search of Excellence*, caught the eye of millions of readers, many of whom are exactly the kind of customers Nordstrom's caters to. The cost of granting the request of one unreasonable customer bought incalculable advertising. Ironically, in some countries, government regulation forbids lifetime guarantees! The American catalog company Lands' End has a simple and reassuring motto for shoppers: *Guaranteed. Period.* Some short-sighted competitors in Germany took Lands' End to court. They claimed this guarantee was unfair advertising and got the court to agree that this guarantee policy was "economically unfeasible" and therefore amounted to unfair competition.

That is a classic case of thinking small and not understanding the value of A-Plus service. Lands' End responded to the court ruling with a set of ads in German newspapers and magazines poking fun at the ban. One ad pictured a common housefly with the caption: *one-day guarantee.* Another showed a washing machine, guaranteed six months. Other companies facing similar bans (Zippo lighters, Tupperware) have dropped their lifetime guarantees but are benefited from the publicity. Zippo ran ads in British papers proclaiming, "A guarantee so good the Germans banned it."[4]

Your company can quibble over guarantees or it can take advantage of A-Plus value perceptions by being generous and open.

Consider calculating the occasional customer who takes unfair advantage of a generous guarantee as a cost of doing business. Pleasantly surprise the large majority of your customers by offering generous guarantee terms. Go beyond what the customer anticipates and reap the reward of customer allegiance.

## Build A-Plus value with goodness of product fit

Goodness of product fit means thinking one-size-fits-*one*. Personalization, not classification into demographic groups, permits real relationship building. The danger of categorizing individuals is illustrated by a letter to the editor of *Fortune*, written by a 13-year-old girl who "often enjoys reading [the] magazine." She was responding to an article called "Girl Power!" in which the magazine described what girls her age were "into." The young lady's articulate response explained that she was not at all like the profile offered in the article. She also criticized *Seventeen, YM, Teen,* and the other magazines that think "much the way you do: that girls can be broken down into a demographic group, that our minds consist of very little more than boys, shopping, makeup, boys, clothes, and shopping."

She goes on to say, "My request to you is that if you are going to say things like this, don't. There is no movie that all girls like, there is no way we all like to dress, there is no music we all like to listen to. It's never fair to make generalizations about any group of people, be it teenage girls or middle-aged business people. Sorry to break it to you, but I am not a demographic group and I don't like your stereotypes, and that is Girl Power!"[5]

Taking the concept of goodness of fit to new levels, *mass customization* is all the rage in manufacturing. Companies are creating products just the way the customer wants them. Levi's can custom-make jeans to the exact measurements of individual customers. The Internet is a popular medium for custom orders. Ford Motor Co. lets buyers "build a vehicle" from a palette of options, while Golf to Fit crafts custom golf clubs based on questionnaire responses. The average person can buy custom clothing at an affordable price, made-to-order music CDs, even personalized vitamins on the Net. Many economists believe that if you don't mass customize, you're going to lose business in today's marketplace.[6]

When companies offer menus of product characteristics for customer to select from, they can create "industrial intimacy." Ultimately, the key is to focus on what is important to the customer and, so long as this still permits the company to make a profit, give customers exactly what they want.

A good friend of mine works as a senior knowledge engineer for a company that sells systems software for customer-relationship management. This CRM[†] software crunches an enormous amount of data and gives specific recommendations for personalizing customer contacts. I can best explain this with a hypothetical example:

Suppose that you are in a financial services business, like a consumer bank or credit union. If your organization is using CRM software, customers who call or visit your office would deal with a person who knows a great deal about them. If George Customer calls your office with a question about his mortgage, your employee would key in the customer's account number. The intelligent systems would display a series of dialogues your employee could use—word for word—to explain customer options and perhaps sell additional products.

The software system gathers and digests mountains of data about the individual customer and about people like him (demographic data). The system may have information about cars he owns, their

---

[†]Customer Relationship Management (CRM) uses various approaches to collect data. Some customers, however, balk at being forced to give companies a lot of personal information. Supermarket preferred-shopper programs that reward customers with discounts when they allow the store to scan a coded card whenever the customer shops are meeting considerable resistance from people who don't want to carry a special card or who resent the deep discounts available only to those who sign up. But companies should be careful to not throw out the baby with the bathwater. Some form of CRM that helps tailor products to individual customers can be very valuable in creating A-Plus value.

price range, and the ages of the cars. It may also factor in data about George such as the fact that he is 55 years old, he is recently divorced, his kids are grown, his mortgage is almost paid off, his Oldsmobile is four years old, and he recently changed jobs after receiving a substantial payout from his previous employer. If you were a financial institution, wouldn't you want to know this?

All this data can suggest additional products we could sell to George. As a result, we build a stronger relationship. We provide A-Plus value by offering products that fit perfectly with this customer's needs. Obviously we benefit, too.

One large mortgage company that uses this advanced contact-management system has had tremendous success in increasing the close rate for additional products. Previously, 4 percent of customers contacting the company purchased additional products. After implementing the system, which provides explicit prompts for customer representatives, the close rate jumped to 38 percent.[7]

The benefit of such additional sales is obvious, but the customer-service element is equally important. This marriage of technology and customer contact builds relationships, enhances customer allegiance, and ultimately builds customer capital.

Sophisticated customer-contact-management products are becoming less expensive and more readily available. Even small businesses can learn more than ever about customer needs, wants, and preferences by gathering appropriate personal data.

To provide A-Plus value, your company may need to be implementing such one-to-one customer service. People don't want to be treated like pieces of demographic data. People often have unique individual needs and wants. A-Plus value is personalized value. It involves doing all you can to be sure the products or services you offer fit the needs of the individual customer, not just some large demographic group.

## Build A-Plus value with memorable experiences

A highlight of many a kid's birthday celebrations has been a trip to a Chuck E Cheese restaurant. These pizza emporiums are something else; they go beyond the traditional description of a restaurant. The food is adequate, but the experience is, well, something kids go nuts over. It's a carnival atmosphere with all kinds of exciting sights and sounds. Providing customers with an *experience* may well be the highest level of economic value. In today's prosperous world, consumers in developed countries have most of the tangible goods they need. Those fortunate enough to benefit from economic good fortune have about all the luxury cars, quality clothes, and trendy coffees they can handle. People today are using more discretionary income to enjoy experiences such as entertainment, travel, cruises, spas, and wellness or retreat centers.

Smart companies are connecting with their customers through experiences. An experience occurs when the company's core products are used as props to engage individual customers in a way that creates a memorable event.[8] Examples of events include live entertainment at restaurants and coffee-shop chats at bookstores. Sporting events and competitions may place the company's products in the background, but the customer receives value from the event itself. Ties to the company are likely to follow.

A word of caution, however: When creating A-Plus value using customer experiences, don't let the core product go bad. Planet Hollywood was a red-hot restaurant chain in the mid-1990s, only to crash when people realized that the glitzy experience of possible celebrity spotting was not worth eating the substandard food. The company largely forgot about its core product—the food.

Experiences can enhance the sense of value so long as the core product maintains its good quality.

## Build A-Plus value with uniqueness and shared values

An enhanced sense of value can stem from a company being perceived as unique or novel. Much of this uniqueness arises from the personality or culture of your organization. Ben and Jerry's ice-cream business projects a sense of culture based on the liberal political values of its founders and its sense of civic responsibility to Vermont. (The ice-cream-plant tours are the most-popular tourist attraction in the state.) Their theme was consistent throughout the history of the company (until it was sold to a large food conglomerate) and had been the subject of books, articles, and television magazine shows.

Southwest Airlines does a good job of conveying a charming quirkiness that reflects its founder, Herb Kelleher. The airline started as a scrappy little outfit and has grown into an aviation powerhouse in part because it customers like the people who work there. SWA hires people based on their upbeat attitudes. The interview process and new-employee orientation is uniquely tailored to help people fit the corporate culture. New employees engage in a scavenger hunt to find answers to company-orientation questions, for example. It is noteworthy that SWA is the only U.S. Airline to be continually profitable in the early years of the '00s.

Ben and Jerry's, SWA, Home Depot, numerous high-tech firms, and many other companies offer their internal customers—their employees—A-plus value by inviting participation in their uniqueness and shared values.

Customers will often go out of their way to support companies that share their values. Talk-show hosts such as Rush Limbaugh, Sean Hannity, and news commentator Paul Harvey have been credited with launching many popular brands because listeners who share their views feel they are getting enhanced value from companies that agree with them.

Political, church, civic, alumni, and charitable groups often band together to promote or support certain organizations. This bonding may range from partnering with credit-card companies to have the organization's logo on the cards, to cell phones with a hockey-team logo, to the purchase of Girl Scout cookies. The opportunity to share in an affiliation, an interest, or a cause is an enhanced sense of value for many people.

On a more-local basis, we become loyal to companies that make us feel comfortable. We patronize organizations that reflect our values and preferences. Even the enormous pricing advantage of the world's big-box discount stores cannot compete with the highly personalized camaraderie of shared values offered when well-run local businesses offer A-Plus value.

## Build A-Plus value with credibility

Customers also feel they are receiving extra value when dealing with companies that have exceptional credibility. A critical dimension of value is the *degree to which customers trust* a company or organization. Failure to follow through on commitments and other deceptive practices can (and should) destroy a company. Of course, sometimes this too is perceptual. You may feel you explained a policy or guarantee to the customer and he interpreted it differently. You think you communicated openly and she sees your limitations as unnecessary fine-print nitpicking.

*Give A-Plus value by keeping pricing and restrictions simple and understandable for customers.* In recent months, competing long-distance telephone companies have made strides to simplify. Most now offer one rate for calls at any time during the day with no hidden charges. It took them a while to get here, but now at least the customer understands and can make a rational choice without fearing deceptive practices. (Now let's hope the cellphone people get a clue.)

The airlines, on the other hand, do a poor job of building credibility with customers and will, I predict, one day pay a price for their evasiveness, their myriad restrictions, and their enormous fare discrepancies. On any given flight, you will find passengers who have paid up to ten times as much as another passenger for the same service: transportation from point A to point B. You may be delighted with your $200 fare, while the guy next to you paid $1,000 or more, depending on when the ticket was booked and a lot of other factors. In short, the airlines' fare systems are unintelligible to their customers and foster a lack of trust.

Speaking of airlines, I also recommend that companies *avoid frequent-flyer-type fiascoes.* Yes, such programs have been successful from a marketing perspective, but they have also been the source of many customer frustrations. Too often, frequent-flyer programs are confusing and often perceived as untrustworthy. While enticing passengers to fly the same airline, the promised rewards come only with a lot of strings attached. Customers who accumulate miles too often find the promised free tickets or service-class upgrades are simply not available. What the airlines do not freely tell is that each flight has only a few award-travel seats. They also don't mention blackout dates, upgrades that cannot be offered from a certain class of tickets, and a lot of other limitations. In short, they shoot their corporate credibility in the foot with lavish promises that are too often not delivered. In fact, seats available for reward travel range from as low as 4.9 percent to 9.8 percent. The average is about 6 percent—six seats out of a hundred.[9] I personally tried to redeem an airlines frequent-flyer seat by booking four months in advance and was told the flight was sold out. A quick check on the Web showed many empty seats on that flight. This does not help credibility. Airlines insist that they are not trying to make it hard to redeem miles for tickets, but with planes carrying record numbers of passengers, the demand for free seats far exceeds the space available.

*Following up on commitments made* is also crucial to building trust with customers. A few years ago, I purchased a rather pricey six-month-old used car from a dealership that touted itself as a no-dicker, full-service auto consortium. Among the many frustrations I experienced, I was given just one key to the car and promised that they would get me another because they had lost the backup. After repeated phone calls, I finally gave up, took the car to another dealership and bought the key—along with several other missing parts like the CD-changer cartridge and all the owner's manuals. I had to go to the right dealership in another city and buy the parts that were missing from my car! The aggravation of getting anything out of that dealership (which, no surprise, has since gone broke) became more than I could handle. I am sure this dealership thinks it won. I quit pestering them, and they didn't have to go out of their way for me. But the price they paid in damaged credibility returned to bite them. I take every opportunity to tell other people (including students in my large university classes) about this poor value experience.

There can be no A-Plus value without credibility. The solutions to the kinds of problems described above are to not offer incentives you cannot provide or to make good on your word. Those are the only choices.

On a more-positive note, we all prefer to do business with people we can trust. I have a scrupulously honest handyman who fixes things around my house. I give him the key to the house so he can go in and work when I am away. I know I can trust him to do good work at a fair price. I have also been blessed with the opportunity of working for high-credibility organizations as an employee. Trust is a powerful form of A-plus value.

## Build A-Plus value with add-ons

One of the simplest ways to surprise customers or employees is to give them something unexpected—or sell them something else they may need. When a shoe-store clerk gives you a shoehorn with a pair of new shoes or when he asks if you'd like to try padded inserts or a pair of lifetime-guarantee socks, he is using this A-Plus value approach. Sometimes add-ons are sold, sometimes given away. Both can be effective. A clerk at a supermarket hands customers a few chocolate kisses with the receipt, an unexpected thank you. The hotel check-in desk has a basket of complimentary apples or a plate of fresh-baked cookies. The paint-store salesperson checks to be sure buyers have caulking and sandpaper.

Employees who receive unexpected small tangible rewards experience A-Plus relationships. A surprise free lunch, a few movie tickets, flowers, impromptu celebrations, and the like all build employee allegiance.

The best kinds of free add-ons are those with high perceived value and low cost to the business. For example, gas stations that give away a free car wash with fill-up are offering something that costs them a few cents (water and soap—not counting, of course, the cost of the equipment), but their customers receive a service with a perceived value of three or four dollars (which is the price printed on the coupon). Free popcorn or drinks given away with video rentals cost three or four cents but have a much higher perceived value. (Really high, when compared to the price of movie-theater popcorn!)

Obviously, this A-Plus opportunity area ties in closely with its marketing counterpart, add-on sales. Marketers have long recognized the value of trying to sell current customers something else so long as they are already buying. This can backfire if it's too pushy, but most customers will not resent low-key inquiries about the need for other products. The hardware salesperson who checks with the customer to be sure he has the right tools is not going to be resented. And the company may well sell some additional products.

One of the more creative add-ons came out of a seminar I ran a few years ago. A woman attending the session owned several quick-lube shops. When we talked about add-ons, she came up with this idea: When people bought a full-service oil change, she did what her competitors had been doing. She checked all fluids, washed windows, checked tire pressure and vacuumed the car's interior. But then she had this add-on idea: She ran a cassette head-cleaning tape through the customer's sound system. We all know that cleaning the cassette tape player this way makes for better sound, but most people never get around to it. After running the cleaning tape, she inserted a preprinted card into the tape player noting that the heads had been cleaned courtesy of her company. This add-on cost practically nothing, but provided a clear and distinctive A-Plus for her customers.

Central to the philosophy of add-ons is the belief that you cannot give away more than you eventually receive. That is a tough concept for people to accept. But, at some philosophical level, you need to be comfortable with the belief that what goes around comes around. In fact, that is fundamental to all the A-Plus allegiance-building tactics. You really will benefit from generosity. Take the leap of faith and reap the rewards of greater customer and employee loyalty.

## A-Plus Value and Employee Allegiance

I have focused mostly on customers in this chapter's discussion, but the principles for creating A-Plus value also apply to employees. Companies with strong employee allegiance regularly use these kinds of ideas to surprise their people—to exceed their expectations with little things.

Virtually every type of A-Plus value can be applied to employee relations with powerful results. Employees who receive small tokens of appreciation respond as positively as do other types of customers. Employees who enjoy the shared experience of working in a good company, who appreciate the credibility of the organization, who recognize the company's efforts to fit people to the best job for them, and who are offered unexpected value will be loyal to the company. Loyal, long-term employees make economic good sense.

Get all members of the organization thinking about ways to utilize little things to create A-Plus value. The payoff in customer and employee allegiance can be enormous.

## Notes

1. B. Joseph Pine II and James H. Gilmore, "Welcome to the Experience Economy," *Harvard Business Review,* July-August 1998, p. 97.

2. Michael Schuman and Hae Won Choi, "Suwon's Restrooms, Once the Pits, Are Flush with Tourists," *Wall Street Journal,* November 26, 1999, p. A-1.

3. Toyota once ran a series of television commercials that showed not their new trucks, but instead a driver stepping out of a ten-year-old model perched on top of a mountain. The actor looks into the camera and announces that he has over 300,000 miles on his truck. Implication: buy a new truck and it'll exceed your anticipated long-term value.

4. "Lands' End Guarantee Verboten in Germany," Salt Lake City, *Deseret News* (AP), September 25, 1999, p. B-1.

5. Brittany Martin, in "Letters to Fortune," *Fortune,* January 12, 1998, p. 19.

6. "Mass Customization Becomes the New Marketing Mantra," *Wall Street Journal,* April 29, 1999, p. A-1.

7. Interview with Randall Myers, Senior Knowledge Engineer, Sterling Wentworth Corporation, Salt Lake City, October 2001.

8. Pine and Gilmore, p. 98.

9. Melynda Dovel Wilcox and Lynn Woods, "Desperately Seeking Seats," *Kiplinger's Personal Finance Magazine,* July 1999, pp. 88-92.

# Chapter 6

# Giving A-Plus Information

> Every product has an informational component, and with that comes an A-Plus opportunity.

## The Way It Is . . .

When I bought an Acura automobile a few years ago, I was introduced to what I call A-Plus information.

Based on my purchasing experience with dozens of cars, I anticipated that the sales person would tell me to read the owner's manual in the glove box to figure out how to use the various accessories and features of the car. Instead, the Acura sales rep spent about 30 minutes with me—after the sale—showing me how each of the car's features worked; where to check the oil; how to find and use the jack, spare tire, and tool kit; and how to maintain the car's finish. He then programmed the radio to my favorite stations. In short, he gave me the detailed information I needed to make the most of my purchase, and he gave me the information using an unexpected medium: personal instruction. This far exceeded any of my previous experiences with auto dealerships.

Another A-Plus-information experience happened a few years ago when my teen-age son had knee surgery. After the surgery, he was referred to a physical therapist. I anticipated that the therapist would show him how to exercise his knees to aid in recovery. She did this, but she also added some small touches I saw as A-Plus. She photocopied pictures of each exercise, wrote his name on the pages in large red letters, taught him each exercise, gave him her home phone number, and encouraged him to call with any questions. She even called him the next day to see how he was doing. Little things? Sure they were. But the composite of these little things went beyond what we had an anticipated and created an A-Plus experience.

The "dot-com" e-tailers are learning about the importance of A-Plus information—and some are doing better than others. A friend's recent online purchase resulted in an unsatisfactory exchange of information. The company sent a message saying the order would be shipped within three or four days; however, the order did not arrive as promised. When the customer inquired about when she could expect to receive the merchandise, she was again told inaccurate information—information that promised shipment that did not happen. A few days later, the customer found the product she ordered (worth several hundred dollars) on her doorstep, having been left out in the rain all night—all this because the company failed to give correct and timely information.

My recent experience with another dot-com merchant also failed badly in the information area. While the company's Web page touted next-day delivery at no extra charge, the merchandise I ordered on Monday still had not arrived on Friday. My email to the company went unanswered. I finally called and was told that part of my order had been shipped and that the back-ordered portion would be shipped in two days. A day later, I received the following email message addressed to "Dear Valued Customer" (shown exactly as I received it):

```
The following item(s) within Your order
#WO3690775 have been updated, and now
have the following status:
SKU # IN-2027      -Processing;
SKU # TQ-1010      -Shipped;
SKU # VS-1135      -Shipped;
SKU # UE-1003      -Shipped;
```

Does this make any sense to you? It sure didn't to me. The company's message uses jargon and numbers that mean nothing to the customer. Customers don't refer to products ordered by SKU numbers, and the status report of "processing" tells nothing. The opportunity to A-Plus customers with useful information is obviously a foreign concept to this company. For that matter, communicating with any clarity also seems unimportant to the company.

In fairness, some e-tailers are getting it right. Online florist Proflowers[†], for example, tells the customer when the ordered flowers were picked up from the distributor, when they were delivered, and even who accepted the delivery. In doing so, ProFlowers is creating the standard in the young and quickly evolving online-business world. Customers are quickly coming to expect that e-tailers will send immediate acknowledgments telling the precise status of their orders, their shipping dates, and costs. Companies that fail to meet this level of service will soon be left in the e-trade dust.

---

[†]My recent experience with ProFlowers reinforced my loyalty. A Christmas-wreath order to my sister in Iowa was scheduled for delivery December 15. ProFlowers called me on the 12th and left a voice message asking me to contact them on their toll-free line. When I did, they apologized profusely for a failure to get the order faxed to their Iowa distributor and advised me the shipment would be one day late. They then waived the shipping charge.

## A-Plus Information: What It Is

Every product, service, or purchasing experience has an informational component. If you buy a can of soup, its label is likely to include nutritional data, preparation tips, and recipes. Vehicles, tools, appliances, and electronic equipment have detailed owner's manuals. Lawn-care services are likely to tell you how often to water or fertilize your grass. Athletic equipment comes with exercise guides or perhaps with a video showing how to get the best results from the product. Customers have come to expect to receive such information.

A company creates A-Plus information by giving information that is more timely, clear, interesting, or creative than is anticipated.

For e-commerce, timely information on the status of customer orders is especially important to retention and loyalty. And sometimes this information is better delivered using a medium other than the Web. A young entrepreneur, Erika Wilde, has a successful online business selling floor mats (www.StopDirt.com). When Erika's customers have questions or if they are making a substantial first-time order, she calls them personally and introduces herself. She supplements the efficiency of the Net with the telephone to build more-personal relationships—thus providing A-Plus information.

Online customers may feel left in a vacuum if the company does not communicate efficiently, clearly, and in a timely manner. *Internet Daily* says that many online brokerages, for example, flunk the service test:

"Online brokerages have a lot of work to do to improve customer service. Researchers at Jupiter Communications tested 25 web sites' rates of response to customers' messages. Among financial-services sites, 39 percent responded in one day, while the balance took up to three days or, in the case of 25 percent, never responded."[1]

As e-commerce becomes more sophisticated, companies are finding ways to respond in more timely and effective ways. The Allegiance Technologies Active Listening System described in Chapter 3 monitors and records responses to customers and employees and assures timely dialogue.

Information handling provides an opportunity to surprise customers. A-Plus information happens when customers receive more timely, clearer, or more useful information than they anticipated. The same applies to employee communication, of course. When workers feel well informed and involved in their company, allegiance increases.

# How to Produce A-Plus Information

Let's look now at some specific ways to create an A-Plus-information experience for customers and employees. This chapter will get you thinking about A-Plus information ideas as I describe uses of informational handholding, media selection, message clarity, information accessibility, and user groups.

## Provide informational handholding

The explosive growth of electronic commerce provides a golden opportunity to use A-Plus information to exceed what customers anticipate. The young and rapidly changing e-commerce world offers a wide range of service levels as many companies work to figure out how to do it well. Customers are just beginning to develop loyalties to certain e-tailers and are bookmarking select Web sites on their computers.

Until customers feel completely comfortable about the information they receive on the Net, they are likely to examine merchandise online and then purchase it off line at brick-and-mortar retailers. Customers say they still aren't filling electronic shopping carts because they don't get enough handholding on the Net.

Indeed, as recently as 1999, research showed that 90 percent of online customers prefer human interaction.[2] We can assume that people are getting increasingly comfortable with e-commerce but that a substantial number who always prefer the kinds of information they get from human contact. Getting useful, reassuring information into the heads of customers should be an important part of the development of any e-commerce efforts.

Opportunities to improve customer handholding isn't just for electronic commerce. Better organizations of all types are increasingly sensitive to customer discomfort and are doing things to reduce it. Companies that have personal guides, personal shoppers, and private bankers are doing additional handholding. Companies that have exceptionally friendly receptionists or greeters who greet and keep customers informed of matters of interest to them are doing handholding. Managers who maintain legitimate open-door policies and are receptive to employee concerns are doing additional handholding. Company leaders who give customers their home phone numbers and invite them to call if they have problems or concerns are doing handholding, too.

Look carefully at your company. Are you providing informational opportunities that make customers and employees comfortable and confident as they do business with you?

## Select informational media carefully

When providing customers with information, consider various media options. Media should be chosen on the basis of communication effectiveness, not just efficiency. Communication *efficiency* is a simple ratio of the costs of communicating relative to the number of people reached by the message. If a message is extremely simple (a no-parking sign, a memo announcing a price change on a particular product, or a simple cooking tip or recipe), we can get away with an efficient medium such as a flier, label, or simple instruction sheet. But as soon as we go beyond such simple messages, communication *effectiveness* becomes more important than *efficiency*.

Communication *effectiveness* is different from communication efficiency. Effectiveness is achieved when the message is

- *received* by the right people (and not others),
- *understood*,
- *remembered* for a reasonable amount of time, and
- *used*.

Effective media are seldom simple or cheap. The greatest effectiveness is typically achieved when people talk face-to-face. This one-to-one communication is, of course, much more expensive (far less *efficient*) than an instruction sheet or owner's manual. But if the message is crucial to the customer's satisfaction with the product, it will be well worth the extra cost. My Acura dealer apparently believed in paying the price for personalized, face-to-face communication when he taught me about the features of my new car.

Much misunderstanding can be attributed to overemphasizing *efficiency* when we should focus on *effectiveness*. Sometimes it doesn't pay to be efficient. The cheap, easy way to give information (for example, the email from the online merchant who identified products only by SKU numbers) doesn't do the job.

Creative companies seek to A-Plus by breaking away from the usual and by using a variety of media for various messages. Chevrolet, for example, goes beyond the owner's manual and provides an audiotape to teach customers how to use the features of their car or truck. Some companies provide videotapes to teach customers how to assemble or use a product. Online help and telephone hotlines (if well designed and responsive) have saved many a frustrated consumer.

Many organizations now have online help services with frequently asked questions (FAQs). The best ones use several levels of FAQs. Some questions address the basic needs of prospects and newer customers. Other FAQs are for experienced customers who know their way around the company's products and services.[3]

In the early days of personal computers, documentation (the instruction manual) was notoriously bad. It was hard to read and often grammatically incorrect. Today's computer or software buyer wouldn't stand for that for a minute. The informational bar has been raised considerably. What passed for the norm in the 1980s would be totally unacceptable in today's plug-and-play world.

Employee communication also poses opportunities for exceeding expectations in information. The best companies to work for typically use active, multi-faceted employee-communication and -training efforts. People are unlikely to be feel allegiance to companies that treat them like hired hands. Great companies hire the whole man or woman. They provide extensive training and information that creates high levels of employee engagement.

Progressive companies are constantly looking for media options that allow them to A-Plus their customers and their employees.

## Constantly strive for message clarity

Regardless of the media used, information must be clear and understandable. Intelligent companies seek clarity by presenting their messages with short, clear sentences, a logical sequence of information, and enough repetition to effectively teach the message receiver.

### Consider an audit of your company's writing

Many organizations could benefit from having a professional business-communication expert audit their written documents, telephone scripts, and presentations. My colleague, Dr. Sherron Bienvenu of Emory University, recently completed a project for an Atlanta company that recognized that its written documents were not the quality they wanted.

Dr. Bienvenu analyzed a sample of the letters and memos sent to the client's customers and quickly recognized some patterns that could be improved on. Among the problems she found are some that you, too, may be experiencing in your documents:

1. *Abrupt tone.* While most readers appreciate business writers getting directly to the point, many of these letters were too abrupt.

2. Use of *clichés or jargon.* Clichés are overused, stale phrases; jargon is specialized language the company may well understand but the customer may not. If you are not sure the customer will know the meaning of a term, use a simpler, clearer description.

3. Use of *stock numbers or abbreviations.* In many cases, the reader may not understand or recognize these.

4. *Failure to express appreciation.* The most powerful phrase in any relationship is probably *thank you.* Instead of telling a reader that his order cannot be shipped as planned, start the message with a thank-you for his order or for his patience.

5. *Failure to offer an alternative* to solve a problem. Don't just tell readers what you cannot do; tell them what you can do.

6. *Failure to provide a reasonable explanation.* Don't say "it's against our policy" and think that does it. Take a moment to explain why the policy is as it is.

As any author would testify, we can always improve the wording of almost anything we write or say. Being willing to edit and re-edit messages is critical to ongoing improvement and the opportunity to create A-Plus information.

## Use some redundancy

People don't always get your messages immediately, and *redundant communication* will help create A-Plus information. For example, you get better results by presenting information both verbally (with words) and graphically (with pictures or diagrams). Likewise, an owner's manual with a supplemental video, reference chart, online help program, or telephone hotline will improve the likelihood of customer satisfaction with a product. Such redundant systems are keys to understanding.

## Make key information easily accessible with graphics and icons

Sometime A-Plus information can be as simple as providing clear signs. I consulted with a hospital that had a rather unusual floor plan. What appeared to be the main entrance opened onto a large foyer area with a reception desk. But because the local folks knew that just about everyone came in through the emergency-room entry, this reception area was not staffed. People unfamiliar with the hospital would come in this front door and have no idea where to go. We improved the signs and added some color-coded strips on the floor to lead to various departments.

Signs can also have marketing and employee benefits as well. One example comes from Wal-Mart pharmacies. Pharmacy employees faced the large burden of stocking all those little bottles, jars, and boxes in perfectly straight rows in aisle after aisle. Every time a customer picked something up to read the label, the display needed to be straightened or the products turned to face front. It was a lot of work. So, Wal-Mart began replacing traditional shelves with a system of bins. Instead of facing a shelf of aspirin bottles, say, the shopper saw a blowup of the aspirin bottle's label. Under that blowup was the bin, into which the aspirin bottles had been dumped.

The enlarged sign provided A-Plus information and solved the problem of stocking—a clerk could just roll a trolley of merchandise to the aisle, open the bin, dump in the goods, and move on. No more need for straight lines of merchandise.

Shoppers liked it better, too. Instead of facing a row of bottles with tiny print, they saw a large, easy-to-read version of the label. It was much easier on the eyes, a special benefit for elderly shoppers.

## Create and support customer user groups and classes

Organizations that bring groups of customers together for user groups are also offering A-Plus information. Such groups are naturals for craft shops, computer stores, financial institutions, and similar organizations and may also work in other arenas. Examples are food stores that offer cooking classes; credit unions that sponsor free classes on investments, budgeting, and personal finance; or auto repair shops that offer classes on auto maintenance.

One of my clients was a medium-sized tire shop and auto-repair business. While brainstorming ideas for giving A-Plus information, the employees decided to offer auto-maintenance classes, specifically tailored to the needs of their female customers. Through some creative advertising and frequent mention of the classes to customers, they got a pretty good turnout. The classes covered tips for tire care, guided tours of a car's exhaust system (with a mechanic showing the parts on a car on a lift), and even a session on maintaining auto paint and upholstery. The groups were small at first but grew as customers became aware that the classes ran every Tuesday evening at 7. And you can bet those who attended the classes were loyal customers.

Motorcycle manufacturer Harley Davidson brings A-Plus service to its customers through its Harley Owners Group (HOG). Started in 1983 in an attempt to stem slipping sales, HOG grew from 33,000 members to about 700,000.

Harley found that people were giving up riding because they didn't have anyone to ride with. HOG brings Harley riders together for rides or to swap tips. "It gives a person a way into a subculture," says Mike Keefe, HOG's director. In a recent *Investor's Business Daily* story, Keefe describes spending eight days riding and camping out with other Harley owners. "In the mornings, I'm standing in line with six other naked men waiting to use a cold shower. You can't get much closer to a customer than that."[4]

Incidentally, Harley buyers get a one-year HOG membership free with their bike purchase. After that, it costs $40 a year. It's common for Harley executives and administrative workers to take part in HOG activities, thus fostering open communication with customers. This is an excellent example of A-Plus information sharing.

Internal customers—employees—can also gain great benefit from user groups. Repair technicians, for example, can be encouraged to create "communities of interest" where they can share tips and ideas. Cross-departmental cooperation can be enhanced by getting to know each other and each other's functions in the company. Often such groups meet informally over lunch or a few beers after work. Enlightened companies encourage and promote such information-sharing activities.

Businesses should try to increase the level of interaction with their customers and employees using any available media. If a business values its customers, it will want to interact with those customers at every conceivable opportunity. Such interactivity can occur in a wide variety of ways.

# Pay Special Attention to A-Plus Information in E-Commerce

As discussed earlier, e-commerce faces some special challenges and opportunities in providing A-Plus information. Two critical actions are to make customer support easily accessible and to honor the customer-feedback loop.

## Make customer support accessible

One of the greatest challenges of business today is providing timely, effective support to customers who have questions. E-commerce is especially vulnerable to complaints of lack of support. Electronic commerce relies heavily on email for communicating with customers—sometimes too heavily.

Julie Schoenfeld, President of Net Effect, a California-based website developer, describes a commonly heard complaint about e-commerce: "that companies by design are leaving their phone numbers off because they don't want to spend money on having someone stand by and answer the phone. . . . Their feeling is 'We ought to be able to answer questions on the Web.'" Indeed, surveys show that 40 percent of companies don't provide an email address for customers to ask questions, and 75 percent don't post phone numbers.[5]

## Honor the customer-feedback loop

A related and all-too-common complaint of e-commerce buyers is the lack of responsiveness when customers do contact the company with a problem. A survey by e-tailer trade group Shop.org showed that about a quarter of shoppers never received a response to an email request for assistance. "It's Retailing 101: Don't ignore your customers," says Mary Helen Gillespie, president of E-BuyersGuide.com. "Plus, it's not just bad business, it's extremely rude even by today's standards."[6]

Making your company more accessible to your customers is an excellent way to exceed customer expectations and to surprise customers with service that's better than they anticipated. But if you offer help lines, be sure they are adequately staffed with knowledgeable people.

# Measure Your A-Plus Information Efforts

Measuring information efforts can assess a company's effectiveness at creating A-Plus service. Two key measures are logging common questions and auditing communication effectiveness.

## Logging common questions (FAQs)

Develop a system for keeping track of common customer questions. If several people are asking the same questions or experiencing similar confusion, you have an information problem. The Allegiance Technologies Active Listening System provides an easy way to capture customer comments and questions. Using ALS, companies have easy access to a complete transcript of customer input and company responses.

This advice applies to all companies, not just the technologically sophisticated. The smallest shop can make notes of recurring customer concerns. However this information gathering is done, managers need to make it worthwhile for employees to record and pass on the customer's feedback. Offer employees incentives for listing and reporting customer comments. Invite customers to tell you what they are thinking either in writing or orally. (Writing inhibits many comments because it is cumbersome for many people to take the time to write. Teach your employees to make notes of customer responses, preferably in front of customers, so that they know they are being heard.)

## Auditing communication effectiveness

A communication audit is a process for determining the quantity and quality of information flowing through the company as well as that coming into the organization from outside stakeholders. Many auditing techniques are used to assess the communicative health of a company. In most cases, it makes sense to hire a communication consultant to do this. An effective consultant will be able to maintain objectivity, pinpoint communication road-blocks, identify overload problems, and assess the effectiveness of the company's formal and informal communication networks.

Measures of internal communication effectiveness reveal a great deal about the status of employee relations. Employees who feel free to communicate and who see that their input is being considered are far more likely to be loyal to the company than are those who feel outside the communication loop. A primary variable in employee motivation is the feeling that their input is being heard.

For additional information on communication audits, see my web site at **www.Dr.Timm.com.**

Overall, surprising customers and employees with A-Plus information is a powerful way to build allegiance. Look carefully at the informational components of all company interactions and find ways to exceed customer expectations—ways to surprise people with better, clearer, more timely, and more interesting information.

## Notes

1. Frank Bamako, "Online Brokerages Flunk Service Test," *Internet Daily* (sponsored by CBS MarketWatch), September 1, 1999.

2. Bill Meyers, "Service with an E-smile," *USA Today*, October 12, 1999, p. B-1.

3. Jim Sterne, *Customer Service on the Internet*, (New York: John Wiley & Sons, 1996), p. 26.

4. Mike Angell, "By Focusing on Customers, Firms Can Boost Shareholder Value," *Investor's Business Daily*, October 11, 2002, p. A-4.

5. Pete Barlas, "Buckle Your Seatbelts, It's a Bumpy Ride," *Investor's Business Daily*, September 15, 1999, p. A4.

6. Quoted in Frank Barnako, *Internet Daily* (sponsored by CBS MarketWatch), September 10, 1999.

# Chapter 7

# Showing A-Plus Personality

> Unexpected kindness is the most powerful, least costly and most underrated agent of human change. Kindness that catches us by surprise brings out the best in our natures.
>
> —Senator Bob Kerrey[1]

## The Way It Is . . .

Allen's father worked his entire career at a large supermarket. Starting as a stock clerk, he advanced in the company and became a store manager, a position he held for many years. He worked very hard and put in long hours. His income was adequate but certainly not as much as he might have made in another line of work. I asked Allen, "Why does a bright and capable man like your dad work so hard and with such undying allegiance for that supermarket? What motivates him to have such allegiance to that company?"

"I've asked him the same questions," Allen said, "and his response is always the same: the people. He enjoys the people he works with and his customers. They are like a big happy family. He eagerly looks forward to each day of work so he can be with his friends."

Many a difficult or unpleasant job is made palatable by the personalities of the people working together. Employees place a great yet often unspoken value on the associations their jobs provide. The most unhappy employees are often the ones who must work in isolation or with people they do not like. Personality of the workforce is a critical element in company culture, and the culture is a major selling point for employee allegiance.

Likewise, customers prefer to do business where the people are fun to associate with. Think of your own behaviors. Do you keep going back to a particular convenience store or restaurant because the people working there are particularly pleasant? Do the people at certain banks or professional-service companies seem unusually attentive or make you feel really good? Do some Web sites or call centers even seem friendlier and easier to use?

*A-Plus personality* is probably what brings you back to those businesses. As with Allen's father, your driving motivation may be that, doggone it, you just like the people.

## What Is A-Plus Personality?

A-Plus personality exceeds what customers expect by giving more caring, pleasant, competent, friendly, and comfortable interactions. Customers and employees prefer to do business where they enjoy the people. Other things being equal, personal rapport can go a long way toward building allegiance.

I recently had lunch at Chicago's O'Hare Airport. What would you anticipate from a busy airport restaurant in a large city? Many people do not associate friendliness with such locations, but I received an excellent service experience. At Wolfgang Puck's restaurant in the terminal, I encountered one of the most pleasant, efficient servers, named Ana. She approached me with a genuine smile and friendly chat. She then recommended an item on the menu, served me promptly, checked back to see if I needed anything else, refilled my soft drink without waiting for me to ask, and personally wrapped the half of the huge sandwich that I couldn't eat. (I ate the rest on the plane, where the food wasn't nearly as good as Wolfgang's.) I really felt that she enjoyed her work and her customers. This woman personified personality and provided service that far exceeded what I anticipated from an airport restaurant in a big city. She provided me with an *A-Plus experience.*

# Communication Principles That Project Personality

Ultimately, a person's personality is made evident by communication behaviors. Some people are unaware that a myriad of small and often subtle communication cues project their personality and affect their customers' experiences. Awareness of three principles of human communication can help us better understand how this process works.

## Communication principle No. 1: Anything can (and will) convey a message

We convey messages to others through both verbal and nonverbal cues. An otherwise friendly and effective verbal greeting or comment can offend a customer because of a single poorly chosen word or phrase that the customer reacts to negatively. Similarly, some employees communicate nonverbally (and usually unintentionally) through body position, posture, facial expression, or tone of voice that they don't care about their customers. My restaurant server at Wolfgang Puck's, on the other hand, conveyed powerful messages with her smile and pleasant conversation.

All of us occasionally communicate the wrong message with our verbal messages or our nonverbal behaviors. A receptionist who bluntly tells callers they must call back later, a salesperson who fails to greet a customer, a fellow worker who shows up late, a repair person who leaves a mess, an employee who looks sloppy or dirty—all communicate something.

## Communication principle No. 2: The receiver of the message determines what it means

Everyone thinks he communicates just fine, but ultimately that judgment lies with the message *receivers*, who decide what messages mean. Good intentions or "what I really meant . . ." doesn't matter. Only the message that is *received* really counts.

Because our communication style is such a deeply personal thing, changing it can be difficult. We communicate in the ways we do because those ways seem to work for us. But the best communicators are those who carefully consider the responses of others and consistently make adjustments based on those responses. The use of feedback is the most important ingredient in communication improvement.

## Communication principle No. 3: Personality is a composite of all communication behaviors

The conclusions people draw about personalities come from a composite of all communication behaviors, and organizational personality is a composite of the personalities of the employees who customers come in contact with. To project a favorable personality, employees and companies need to be cognizant of the kinds of cues people are paying attention to. And then they need to work toward projecting the most positive messages.

The remainder of this chapter looks at some of the kinds of specific behaviors that communicate meaning to customers and employees. This discussion is by no means an exhaustive list of behaviors, but it does reflect everyday actions that can go a long way toward building customer allegiance.

# How to Project A-Plus Personality

Wal-Mart founder Sam Walton understood organizational behavior when he said, speaking to managers about their employees, "Your people will treat your customers the way you treat your people." Enthusiasm, comradeship, a sense of enjoyment, and humor quickly become evident to customers. Southwest Airlines, which has a culture of informality and fun at work, projects an organizational personality very different from many of its competitors. This personality has been useful in attracting both customers and employees.

As you read this chapter and become aware of some key behaviors used by individuals and organizations to convey personality to customers and employees, you'll quickly recognize A-Plus opportunities in each.

As you discover some of these ideas, you may say, "Well, duh! . . . of course you should do that." But if you haven't thought about some of these details (and many people don't), your new awareness alone can dramatically improve the ways you project personality.[2]

## Build A-Plus personality by treating people like guests

The first few seconds of an encounter with a customer or employee can set the stage for an ongoing relationship. Here are some ways to get off on the right foot—

### Greet people promptly

Woody Allen once said that 80 percent of success is just showing up. In customer service, 80 percent of success is treating the customer like a guest who just showed up.

When guests come to your home, you greet them, right? Yet we've all had the experience of being totally ignored by service people in some businesses. It feels awkward and quickly becomes annoying.

A prompt greeting reduces the stress people feel when they find themselves on unfamiliar turf. Failing to greet would be like answering the doorbell at home, opening the front door, letting a guest into the foyer, and walking away without even acknowledging him. Anyone would feel awkward and uncomfortable in such a situation.

Studies have clocked the number of seconds customers waited to be greeted. Researchers then asked the customer how long they'd been waiting. In every case, the customer's estimate of the time elapsed was much longer than the actual time. A wait of 30 or 40 seconds felt like three or four minutes.

I once went to a watch repair shop where the repairman had a reputation for excellent work. His shop was tiny. I literally had to squeeze in behind another customer who was talking with the proprietor, who never looked at me, said hello, or acknowledged my presence. After a few minutes, I decided to "come back later" because it felt awkward to wait in the shop while being ignored. Of course, I didn't go back, and the repairman lost a customer simply because he failed to greet me.

Without prompt, friendly greetings, customers are unlikely to feel comfortable. So, speak up. Verbally greet people within a few seconds of the time they come into your business or approach your work location. Even if you are busy with another customer or on the phone, pause to say hello and let them know that you'll be ready to help them soon.

If you absolutely cannot say hello out loud, make eye contact. Simply looking at the person creates a bond between you and the customer. It conveys your interest in communicating further.

### Get your customer committed

A busy fast-food restaurant sends a clerk out to write customers' orders on a sheet of paper while they are waiting in line. Customers tell the clerk what they want, and he or she marks it on a slip of paper, which is then given back to the customer to present at the cash register, where the order is called out. Why do they do this? It is simply a way of getting the customer committed. If no one greeted customers or wrote their orders, they may be more likely to leave. Psychologically, they feel like they've "ordered," so they stay in line and follow through with their meal purchase.

Another way to get customers committed is to get them doing something. Telling customers about your products or services isn't enough. They need to be doing something. Successful computer salespeople, for example, encourage customers to sit down at the computer as soon as possible to get them playing with it. The sales reps don't dazzle (or confuse) the customer with high-tech jargon or even information about the machine's capabilities. They get them *doing something*. Likewise, great automobile salespeople invite customers to sit in or test drive the car right away.

Here are some other ways to get people doing something:

- Personally hand them a shopping cart or basket
- Ask them to begin filling out paperwork
- Get them to touch or sample the product
- Offer a cup of coffee, candy, or fruit while they wait
- Give them a product flier, information packet, video presentation, or sample to review

It doesn't matter so much *what* they do, so long as they begin to do *something*.

## Build A-Plus personality by developing rapport

Once you have greeted the customer, build rapport. Project your favorable personality with the following communication behaviors.

### Smile sincerely and openly

A genuine smile originates in two places, the mouth and the eyes. A lips-only version looks pasted on, insincere. It's like saying "cheese" for a photograph. It doesn't fool anyone, and, in fact, it might scare them away.

In fairness, some people smile more readily than others. For some, a more serious facial expression is comfortable and natural. But in North American cultures, a smile is both expected and appreciated when one is meeting people. If you don't smile spontaneously, practice it. Your smile need not be a Cheshire cat, ear-to-ear grin (in fact, that may really get people wondering about you), but just a pleasant, natural smile.

Incidentally, in some cultures smiling means something different. In Israel, for example, a clerk who smiles at customers is generally perceived as being inexperienced; in some middle-Eastern cultures, smiling is associated with a sexual come-on. But for most cultures, smiling is a rapport builder.

### Break the ice

The best way to start a conversation depends on what the other person needs. In many cases, customers or employees need first to be reassured that you are a good person and that the organization is a nice, friendly place to do business. They need to dispel worries about being pressured into something they don't want to do. To do so, use a non-threatening conversation starter.

Often customers want to browse or "get the feel of the place" before they commit to doing business. A good icebreaker for such situations can be an off-topic, friendly comment. Some options might be:

- A compliment ("That's a great-looking tie/scarf/coat." "Nice office." "Your children sure are cute. How old are they?")

- Weather-related or local-interest comments ("Isn't this sunshine just beautiful?" "Some snowfall, isn't it?" "How about those Bulls last night?")

- Small talk. Look for cues about the person's interests in sports, jobs, mutual acquaintances, past experiences, and so on. Then initiate a relevant comment.

If the person seems to be focusing attention on a product (say he is holding several shirts or is looking at a particular line of products), he can be reclassified as a *focused shopper*. The best icebreaker for the focused shopper is one that is more specific to the buying decision. It may:

- Anticipate the customer's questions ("What size are you looking for, sir?" or "Can I help you select a —?")

- Provide additional information ("Those are all 25 percent off today." Or "We have additional — that I can get you.")

- Offer a suggestion or recommendation ("Those striped suits are really popular this season." "If you need help measuring the job, our estimators can figure out what you'll need.")

In non-retailing organizations, use friendly, sincere expression of willingness to serve. Ask: "How can I help you?"

## Compliment freely and sincerely

It takes only a second to say something nice to a person, and it can add enormous goodwill. As with the icebreaker, you may comment on something they are wearing, their car, or their children. When you talk with employees, complimenting their work effectiveness or expressing appreciation can be a good way to build rapport. ("Thanks for waiting. You've been very patient." "I noticed you checking the —. You're a careful shopper." "You seem to know a lot about —. Let's see if we can meet your needs." "I appreciate the way you handled the Murphy account.")

In short, you can get a lot of mileage out of complimenting people freely and sincerely. Try this: Set a goal to give ten sincere compliments each day. Make it a habit. This is a powerful way to project A-Plus personality.

## Call people by name

A person's name is his or her favorite sound. We appreciate it when people make the effort to find out and use our name in addressing us. When appropriate, introduce yourself to customers and ask for their names. If this isn't appropriate (such as when you are waiting on a line of customers), you can often get customers' names from their checks, credit cards, order forms, or other paperwork. Make an effort to learn the names of employees and associates.

When dealing with customers, don't be overly familiar too quickly. You are normally safe calling people *Mr. Smith* or *Ms. Jones*, but you may be seen as rude if you call them *Homer* and *Marge*. (This is especially true when younger employees are dealing with older customers.) Better to err on the side of being a bit too formal rather than risk seeming disrespectful. If people prefer first-name address, they'll tell you so.

### Be sensitive to timing and follow-up

Nothing impresses as significantly as immediate follow-up. If you commit to something for a customer or employee, do it and do it promptly. If you are serious about creating positive relationships with customers and employees, follow up to be certain they are satisfied. Follow up on all commitments.

I have an insurance man who calls me every year on my birthday and on my wedding anniversary. He *never* fails. And, although it's become a joke in our family that we'll hear from Ray on that day, he has been absolutely consistent for almost 20 years! That tells me something about his commitment to long-term relationships with his customers.

### Reach out and touch customers

Physical touch is a powerful form of communication. Take an opportunity to shake hands with people or pat them on the back, if appropriate.

A study of bank tellers shows the power of touch. Tellers were taught to place change in the hand of the customer rather than place it on the counter. Researchers found that customer perceptions of the bank rose sharply among customers who had been touched. In a similar study, the Waiter's Association tells members they can increase their tips by 42 percent by touching diners briefly on the shoulder when placing the tip tray on the table or on the palm when returning change.[3]

Among employees and co-workers, a literal pat on the back can build instant rapport. But don't overdo it—some people resent people who seem too touchy-feely. Recognize different preferences; try touching behavior, but be willing to adjust if the person seems uncomfortable or ill at ease. And, of course, keep any touching appropriate. Never touch a person in a manner that could be interpreted as overly intimate or having sexual overtones.

## Build A-Plus personality by creating a communication circle

Good communication is circular and ongoing, not one-directional and sporadic. I discussed in earlier chapters the importance of getting frequent real-time feedback using the Allegiance Technologies Active Listening System. I am convinced that this is an incredibly effective way to create communication dialogues, especially when people have access to technology. In addition to ALS, we can use some informal processes to get feedback and to build strong relationships with customers and employees. Try these tactics:

### Often ask, "How'm I doing?"

Legendary politician and former New York City mayor Ed Koch would constantly ask his constituents. "How'm I doing?" The phrase became his tag line. Apparently he even listened to their answers. After all, he survived as mayor of the Big Apple for many years. We can learn something from the Koch question. Ask it often.

## Listen with more than your ears

Since so few people are really good listeners, this skill provides an excellent A-Plus opportunity. There is no such thing as an unpopular listener. Almost everyone becomes more interesting when they stop talking and start listening. Pay attention to your talk-listen ratio. Are you giving the other people at least equal time? You probably should be.

To be a better listener, use these ideas, and teach them to your employees:

- *Judge the content* of what people are saying, *not the way they are saying it.* Customers may not have the "right" words, and they may not use the same terms you would, but they know what they need better than anyone. Mentally translate their ideas and act on them.

- *Hold your fire.* Don't jump to make judgments before the other person has finished talking.

- *Work at listening.* Maintain eye contact and discipline yourself to listen to what is being said. Tune out thoughts that get you thinking about something else.

- *Resist distractions.* Make the other person the center of your attention. Look at him or her and work to focus on the message.

- *Seek clarification* so you fully understand their needs. Do this in a non-threatening way using sincere, open-ended questions.

## Say *please, thank you,* and *you're welcome*

Be polite. It may seem old-fashioned, and some customers may not be as polite to you, but that's not *their* job.

I have recently seen a disturbing trend among salespeople who say "there you go" to conclude a transaction. That kind of comment is not an appropriate substitute for thanking the customer.

"Thank you" has long been recognized as one of the most powerful phrases in human communication.

Another phrase has taken the place of "you're welcome" for many people. They say "no problem." I recommend sticking with "you're welcome" rather than even implying that the customer caused you a potential problem.

### Reassure the customer's decision to do business with you

Buyer's remorse can set in pretty fast when people make large purchases or important decisions. At the time of sale, you can inoculate against remorse by reassuring the customer that they've made a good purchasing decision.

Phrases like, "I'm sure you'll get lots of enjoyment out of this" or, "Your family will love it" can help reassure and strengthen the buyer's resolve to follow through with the purchase and, just as important, feel good about it.

## Build A-Plus personality with good telephone techniques

Many customer and employee interactions begin with phone contact. To best project A-Plus personality over the telephone, we need to be aware of its strengths and limitations. Below are some tips for making the most of the phone.

### Use effective telephone behaviors

Using the telephone requires some special behaviors, especially if your only contact with customers is by phone. A key to successful phone use is to simply *remember that your customer cannot see you.* Your challenge is to make up for all that lost visual nonverbal communication by using your voice effectively. Here is a review of a few key behaviors:

- *Give the caller your name.* Let the caller know who you are, just as you would in a face-to-face situation (with a name tag, desk plaque, or business card).

- *Smile into the phone.* Somehow people can hear a smile over the phone. Some telephone pros place a mirror in front of them while they're on the phone to remind them that facial expression can be transmitted to their listeners.

- *Keep your caller informed.* If you need to look up information, tell callers what you are doing. Don't leave them holding a dead phone with no clue as to whether you are still with them.

- *Invite the caller to get to the point.* Use such questions as "How can I assist you today?" or "What can I do for you?"

- *Commit to requests of the caller.* Tell the caller specifically what you will do and when you will get back to them. ("I'll check on this billing problem and get back to you by five this afternoon, okay?")

- *Thank the caller.* This lets the caller know when the conversation is over.

- *Let your voice fluctuate in tone, rate, and loudness.* You hold people's attention by putting a little life into your voice. Express honest reactions in expressive ways. Let your voice tones be natural and friendly.

- *Use the hold button carefully.* People hate being put on hold. When it's necessary, explain why, and break in periodically to let them know they haven't been forgotten. If what you're doing will take longer than a few minutes, ask the caller if you can call them back. *Write down your commitment to call back, and don't miss it.*

- *Use friendly, tactful words.* Never accuse the customer of anything; never convey that their request is an imposition.[4]

## Build A-Plus personality by enjoying people

The best service personalities convey a sense of enjoyment in their interaction with people. Yes, customers and employees can be annoying at times, and sometimes personalities do clash, but, people are generally pleasant and interesting. Look for the positive in your association with others.

## Enjoy people and their diversity

J. D. Salinger said, "I am a kind of paranoid in reverse. I suspect people of plotting to make me happy." With an attitude like that, we'd look forward to every meeting with every customer. Of course, we quickly learn that some customers do not seem to be plotting to make us happy. Most are very pleasant; some are unusual. A few are downright difficult.

Every person is different; each has a unique personality. But the kind of people who tend to bug us the most are the ones who are *not like us*. Accept this diversity and learn to enjoy it. Know that peoples' needs are basically the same at some level and that treating them as guests will create the most goodwill, most of the time.

## Work on verbal discipline

Confine your self-talk and your comments to others to positive, upbeat thoughts that avoid being judgmental. Instead of saying, "This kid has a really stupid haircut," avoid commenting at all or say, in a nonjudgmental way, "Kids seem to enjoy looking different." Instead of saying, "This guy seems a few fries short of a happy meal," say "I better take some time to explain my information very carefully."

At times, you'll have to force yourself to avoid the negative and the judgmental. Try making a game out of it. Sincerely try for one full day to *avoid saying anything negative or judgmental* about another person. If you make it through the day, try another day. Verbal discipline can become a habit that pays off. You'll find yourself enjoying people more.

## Build A-Plus personality with organizational culture

In addition to the individual behaviors described above, group behaviors and attitudes project the personality of the entire organization. The communication rule that anything can and will communicate still applies for these behaviors, of course. If the customer likes your culture, you are well on your way to A-Plus personality and to building allegiance. Here are some organizational behaviors to consider.

### "Friendliness" of organizational systems

*Fortune* magazine columnist Stewart Alsop tells of spending 45 minutes buying an upgrade to a plane ticket on America West Airlines. He wanted to pay extra for first-class seats for himself and his wife. The upgrades cost $250 each, but "required the full attention of one of the two gate clerks, as well as assistance from the gate supervisor. Everyone else on the plane had to check in with the one other gate attendant, a process that—of course—took twice as long as usual. As they waited in line, they all could see that I was the one holding things up."

Alsop goes on to describe how the gate agent could not figure out how to respond to his request for the upgrade. She spent considerable time typing mysterious commands into her computer terminal and then talking to the terminal when it didn't do what she hoped it would. The gate supervisors had to help, and the process even involved filling out carbon-copy forms to serve as credit-card receipts. Alsop summarizes the irony of the episode:

"Think about this: I was a customer who wanted to pay an extraordinarily high price (almost twice the original fare) for something that costs the airline little more than the price of a better snack. . . . I wanted to pay an extra $500 for the privilege of sitting in seats that, as it turned out, would have been empty anyway. The airline's response to this opportunity? Forcing me to stand in line and making me feel like a blithering idiot in front of my friends and spouse."[5]

Clumsy systems turn off customers and communicate unspoken messages. In this case, the customer received the message that he was a troublesome burden.

## The company's appearance and grooming

From the moment we meet people, we begin to size them up. We begin to draw conclusions about them almost immediately. What we decide about their trustworthiness and ability is largely a factor of first impressions, and, of course, you only get one chance to make that first impression.

The appearance of an organization's employees is one of the first things seen by customers. Dress standards can set a company apart from the competition and create an A-Plus experience.

An owner of an auto repair shop tried an experiment. Each of his repair people was paid on commission for the amount of repair work they brought in. He invited the mechanics to volunteer to change their dress and grooming. Several agreed to cut their hair shorter, shave daily, and wear clean uniforms. The outcome was a good example of A-Plus: Those who improved their appearance generated far more repeat business than the others. The customers would ask for the better-dressed mechanics, and those who chose to dress and groom themselves in the old ways found themselves getting less work.

Remember, of course, that the key word in dress and grooming is *appropriate*. Salespeople in a surf shop would look foolish in three-piece suits; an undertaker would look ludicrous in surfer shorts.

To overcome problems of individual differences that may be inappropriate, some organizations issue uniforms. These may be coveralls, full uniforms, or partial uniforms, such as blazers, vests, or work shirts. Some employees like these (they save on the costs of a wardrobe), while some resist the sameness of the uniformed look.

Determine what level of professionalism you want your people to convey to customers, and then create a look that projects competence. Your customers notice these things.

## Check the appearance of work areas

A cluttered work area conveys a sense of disorganization and lack of professionalism. Look around you and see what your customer sees. Is the place clean and tidy? Does the workspace look like an organized, efficient place? Is merchandise displayed attractively? Is an office attractively furnished?

Check, too, for barriers. People often arrange their work space with a desk, counter, or table between them and the customer. While sometimes this is necessary, it often creates a barrier—both physical and psychological—between the customer and the employee. Invite customers or employees to sit beside your desk instead of across from you. Consider using small round tables, especially when customers need to read materials you give them. Some auto dealerships have removed all sales-office desks and replaced them with small round tables. Now the customer and salesperson sit around the table and work together to make a deal. Seated at a round table with the salesperson, customers don't feel like they are on opposite sides, in "combat" with each other.

Finally, consider customer comfort. Are your customers invited to sit in a comfortable chair? Do your offices or stores invite them to relax? Are waiting areas furnished with reading materials, music, or perhaps a TV? Are vending machines or refreshments available? Is the vending area kept clean?

Recently, more auto dealers have begun to emphasize ways to make their car lots and showrooms, many of which are decades old, more attractive and customer friendly. Some now feature landscaped settings with benches and pathways, different display areas for each auto brand, and interactive systems with screens that show how elements like paint colors and upholstery look together. Take a look at your work areas from the customer's viewpoint.[6]

## Organizational listening

At the risk of getting repetitious, I want to again stress the need for listening and feedback in winning allegiance. Companies that listen well *A-Plus* their customers with positive organizational personality. A-Plus listening happens when companies:[7]

- *Solicit feedback.* The most valuable feedback we get is the customer complaint. While most people don't like being criticized, the fact is that only through such criticism can meaningful changes be made. A-Plus companies do a good job of soliciting feedback—especially complaints—on product and service quality.

- *Expand market research.* Although companies traditionally invest significantly in this area, they often overlook two critical listening points. Customers should be interviewed both at the time of arrival (when they become customers) and at the time of departure (when they defect) about the reasons for their behavior. A-Plus companies ask customers about their needs, how they heard about the company, what characteristics are they looking for in a company "like ours," and what sparked their decision to use the company's products. Careful questioning of departing customers can isolate the attributes that are causing customers to leave and can demonstrate goodwill by making last-ditch attempts to keep the customer. One company found that it recaptured a full 35 percent of its defectors just by contacting them and listening to them earnestly.7

- *Train and reward front-line employees.* Employees who have direct contact with customers provide a superb way of organizational listening. Train people to listen effectively (do not assume people can do this spontaneously) and to make the first attempts at amends for the customer who has a bad experience.

- *Involve the customer.* Customers who engage in experiences with the company feel a part of the action and feel listened to. Southwest Airlines invites frequent fliers to its first round of interviews with prospective flight attendants and considers those customers' opinions in the hiring process. Creative companies invite prospective customers to participate in new-product development sessions. This is a powerful form of listening that projects an A-Plus personality.

### Regular communication

Use routine notes of thanks to keep communication channels open. Examples: A week after purchasing running shoes, customers of a small shop receive a handwritten note from the store owner simply thanking them for buying. No fancy prose, the note expresses appreciation for their business and invites them to return—a one- or two-sentence message.

An airport car-rental agency has employees write thank-you notes to customers when the desk is not busy. The notes are handwritten on the company letterhead and personalized to mention the type of car rented. They thank customers and invite them to rent again the next time they are in town. The cost of doing this is practically nil, since the desk is busy when flights are coming in but then has slow periods between flight arrivals. Why have employees waste time when business is slow? Use that time to communicate with customers. A quick thank-you is always appreciated.

Other ways to keep communication open are to send customers information about upcoming sales, changes in policies, new promotions, and so on. A print shop sends all customers a monthly package of coupons, fliers, and samples, including a printed motivational quote on parchment paper suitable for framing. Additional copies of the quote are available free for the asking. The mailing acts as a reminder of the quality of work the shop can do, as well as a promotion. Keep the customer tied in with mailings, email updates, or phone contact.

## Stay close after the sale

Customers hate a love-'em-and-leave-'em relationship, yet many companies offer just that. Once the sale is made, the customer goes back to feeling like a stranger. Likewise, employees want constant communication to feel that they are in the know. Look for opportunities to contact people. Examples:

- Add customers and employees to email distribution lists

- Generate newsletters or brief updates about the company

- Call or email to be sure the product or service met their needs

- Send newspaper or magazine clippings of interest

- Send unexpected greeting cards

- Invite people to participate in focus groups

- Call to thank customers for referrals

## Hoopla and fun

People enjoy working in organizations where they have fun. Successful companies have regular rituals, whether they be Friday-afternoon popcorn, birthday parties, or employee-of-the-month celebrations that everyone gets involved in. Excellent organizations are fun places to work; they create rituals of their own.

As a manager at a utility company, I initiated frequent sales contests, complete with skits and prizes. Each time a particular product was sold, the service representative could pop a balloon and find inside a prize ranging from a $10 bill to a coupon good for a piece of pie in the company cafeteria. Employees loved it and got involved.

Other ideas:

- Recognition for employees (or heroes) of the week or month

- Awards luncheons (include some tongue-in-cheek "awards")

- Win a day off with pay (for some special effort)

- Casual-dress days
- Family picnics

Don't think these kinds of things are hokey. Employees at all levels enjoy celebrations and hoopla, and their effects spread to the customer.

## Build A-Plus personality by developing and rewarding employees

Each year *Fortune* magazine puts out an issue highlighting the best companies to work for. One of the key factors in grading companies is the amount of training provided to employees. Training and development is widely regarded as a form of reward for the people who work at an organization. People enjoy learning new things and growing in competency.

Other ideas for building A-Plus personality by developing and rewarding employees include—

### Hiring smart

Employees project organizational personality to customers and associates. No decision is more important to a company than hiring the right people. Hire and promote people on the basis of their attitude and people skills. You can always teach people the technical skills needed to do a job. The people skills are tougher.

When you come across people who just naturally seem to click with other people, make a note to contact them about possible work with you. Make shopping for employees an ongoing activity.

### Rewarding the right actions

Fairly often, organizations inadvertently reward one behavior while hoping for something else. In all too many cases, an organization *hopes* something will happen but actually rewards an opposite behavior. For example: A company rewards individuals and departments for never receiving complaints. The hope is that receiving no complaints means no one is dissatisfied. The reality, however, may be that no complaints are heard because the complaints are being suppressed. Customers have no effective way to voice a complaint. Instead, they just quit doing business with the company.

As we discussed earlier, it's not bad news to receive a complaint; it *is* bad news to suppress a complaint. Some percentage of customers will always be less than satisfied, and ignoring them does no good. Instead, it makes sense to draw out customer concerns so that they can be addressed and corrected.

Here are some other examples of possible conflicts where the wrong behaviors may be rewarded and the right behaviors ignored:

- Rewarding employees for fast transaction handling when the customer may be left uninformed or may resent being rushed along. Examples: The restaurant that encourages employees to get the customer fed and out of the restaurant may create unhappy customers who prefer to eat more slowly. The buyer who does not understand how to work the features of a product he bought may be frustrated when he tries to use the product.

- Encouraging salespeople to cooperate with each other to best meet customer needs while paying a straight commission. Example: Salespeople practically trip over each other to approach new customers before the other salesperson gets them.

- Encouraging employees to send thank-you notes to customers but never allowing on-the-job time to do so. This creates the impression that it really isn't that important.

- Constantly stressing the need to reduce the amount of return merchandise by docking the pay of clerks who accept too many returns. Result: Customers encounter reluctance to take back unsatisfactory products.

- Paying people by the hour instead of by the task accomplished. Hourly wages are simpler to administer, but they basically pay people for using up time.

Any organizational reward system needs to be tilted to the advantage of the employee who supports an excellent culture and provides excellent service. Management is limited only by its imagination when it comes to rewarding employees. But the most important point is that managers must reward the right actions and results.

## A Final Thought

Individual and organizational behaviors are conveyed to customers and employees by little things. People are often unaware of how they are coming across and, as a result, are at a disadvantage. Broadening our awareness of how other people read our verbal and nonverbal messages is useful in improving customer and employee allegiance.

## Notes

1. Kerry was quoted in *Parade*, May 12, 2002, p. 17.

2. Many of the ideas in this section are adapted from Paul R. Timm, *50 Powerful Ideas You Can Use to Keep Your Customers*, 3rd ed., (Hawthorne, NJ: Career Press, 2002). Copyright Paul R. Timm.

3. "TippingTips," *Wall Street Journal*, August 27, 1996, p. A-1.

4. An excellent 30-minute videotape training program featuring the author is *Winning Telephone Techniques*, produced by JWA Video in Chicago. For information, call (312) 829-5100.

5. Alsop, Stewart, "My Trip on America West, Or Why Customer Service Still Matters," *Fortune*, November 22, 1999, p. 359.

6. "A Picnic in a Car Lot?" *Wall Street Journal*, October 13, 1994, p. A-1.

7. Ideas were adapted from Thomas O. Jones and W. Earl Sasser, Jr., "Why Satisfied Customers Defect," *Harvard Business Review*, November-December 1995, p. 93.

8. Jones and Sasser.

# Chapter 8

# Giving A-Plus Convenience

More than ever, 21st century people recognize that time is much more than money. Time is our single most valuable commodity—it is the stuff of life. And companies or people who waste our time are not viewed with appreciation. A Web page that does not open within a few seconds is quickly passed; a service that takes "too long" is avoided; paperwork that is cumbersome and confusing is tossed aside; a company that works too slowly is replaced by one that provides goods and services now!

## The Way It Is . . .

Marcia was a regular customer at the Perimeter Center Publix Supermarket in Atlanta. During the busy Christmas holiday season, she discovered a delicious, low-fat eggnog. But after trying it, she came back for more, only to discover the store was out.

A chat with the dairy-section employee brought promises that more eggnog would be coming in soon. But when she returned to the store a day later, the product was again out of stock. This time the employee said, "More is coming in tomorrow, and I'll set some aside for you." When she returned the next day, the delivery truck had been late, and again she got no eggnog.

This time, the employee offered her A-Plus convenience. He apologized and told her that as soon as the delivery came in, he would set some aside for her and *deliver it to her home* on his way home from work!

Home delivery! What a concept. A generation ago, home delivery of milk and other products was commonplace. In the early 21st century it may be making a comeback.

Online grocery-delivery services and online subsidiaries of many major supermarket chains are re-introducing consumers to a level of convenience not often found in today's business world. According to Louise Lee, writing in *Business Week* online, "Although these companies experienced a significant shakeout when the dot-com bubble burst, the online grocery industry is rising again, thanks mainly to old-line brick-and-mortar chains. [These companies] view home delivery as a way to court their affluent customers and as a rare advantage over discounter Wal-Mart Stores Inc., which is rapidly expanding its grocery business but does not sell food online."[1] A host of big, publicly traded grocery chains are now mounting their own e-grocery experiments or helping fallen dot-coms deliver the goods. "It's not a question of if this will happen. It's when," says Vic Orler, partner in the consumer-goods and -services practice at consultancy Accenture. "Talk to people who have used any of the services. They love it. A lifestyle once expanded is not easily contracted."[2]

Enhancing speed and convenience for customers is a critical tactic for building allegiance. E-commerce sites live and die by their speed and responsiveness. Traditional businesses build great allegiance among customers who value the ways they respect their time and try to provide easy shopping.

# What Is A-Plus Convenience?

Customer and employee convenience arises from speed of service and from ease of doing business. Organizations that strive for levels of efficient, easy-to-use services that exceed people's expectations can use those competitive advantages to capture customer allegiance.

Let's look at the first component of A-Plus convenience: speed. Surpassing what people anticipate about speed may be one of the simplest yet most powerful ways of building allegiance. The ubiquitous convenience store personifies key elements that can be applied to other businesses. C-stores allow parking at the door, reasonable selection, quick self-service, and out-the-door-in-a-minute service. Pay-at-the-pump gas dispensing makes things even quicker for such stores.

The reason people like convenience stores is simple—people value their time, perhaps more than ever before. Unfortunately, aside from convenience stores, many companies are far too casual about wasting customers' time.

We live in a world of commerce where we expect nearly instant gratification. Customers want things free, perfect, and now. We see things on the Web, order them, and fully expect that they will arrive on our doorstep in a day or two. When they do, we are likely to reorder; if they fail to make the promised deadline, we are likely to be disappointed and will quit shopping with that company in favor of one that hustles a bit more.

Despite this customer demand for timely service, many companies still fall into the trap of over-promising and under-delivering. They make vague or unfulfilled commitments involving their customers' time. A few examples:

- A major computer distributor in Europe told the customer that its mainframe would be restored to service "soon." The customer thought "soon" meant 20 minutes or so; to the technician, "soon" meant about 8 hours.

- Some phone or cable companies routinely tell customers that they will be at the customers' homes to install service "between 7:30 a.m. and 5 p.m." on a given date. The customer is expected to sit around all day, waiting for the installation.

- A medical clinic's most common complaint was that patients had to wait too long to see the doctor. Customers felt that doctors had little regard for the value of their time. The result was a negative spiral, where patients showed up later than the appointment time, figuring that the doctor would be late. The clinic then scheduled even more slack into the system, and the situation got worse.

- An online retailer makes a big deal of offering overnight shipment of products so the customer will have them the next day (at no extra charge, according to one promotion). But the merchandise doesn't show up for five days, and the opportunity to A-Plus a customer is long gone. So is the customer, in many cases.

On a more positive note, a number of businesses are built on the simple premise of giving A-Plus speed and convenience by under-promising and over-delivering. Federal Express promises package delivery "by 10:30 a.m.," while it knows it can have the package delivered by 9:30 or 9:45. Customers are routinely surprised because most businesses fail to meet their own deadlines, thus showing a disrespect for the customer's time. A Xerox Corporation branch office used a similar practice. When customers called for a technician to fix their copy machine, they were promised that someone would be at their office by 2 o'clock—when Xerox knew the rep would be there by 1:30 or so. This never failed to pleasantly surprise clients.

The Disney amusement parks create A-Plus speed by having signs showing how long it will take to get to the ride from a given point in line. They have actually scheduled a little "fat" in the estimated wait times. The lines inevitable move more quickly, and customers are pleasantly surprised when a "12-minute wait" is actually just 9 minutes or so. Similarly, restaurants that tell patrons a table will be available in 15 minutes and then seat them in 10 will be far more popular than one promising 15 minutes and delivering 18- or 20-minute seating.

## How to Produce A-Plus Convenience

We can provide A-Plus convenience and speed by making several actions part of our ongoing ways of doing business: (1) seriously value our customers' (and employees') time, (2) make things easier for people, (3) create once-and-done service, (4) make doing business with us easy, (5) offer ancillary services, and (6) simplify the product.

As with any A-Plus tactic, companies need to be ever-vigilant to ways of improving systems and behaviors that can enhance convenience. If you don't offer better and better convenience, your competition will. Customers are screaming for it, and you need to provide it.

### Give serious regard to people's time and convenience

Time is a valuable commodity to our customers and employees. When we disregard it or fail to share their sense of urgency, we discount our customer. Few things are more frustrating than waiting for something that seems to take longer than necessary. In fact, of all the pet peeves identified in my research and described by seminar participants, slow service is at or near the top of everyone's list.

Speed is easier to work with than convenience. In fact, the nice thing about creating A-Plus speed is that you have a lot of control. You can clearly create the expectation by telling customers how long things will take. Once the customer anticipates a particular time period, you can simply beat it, thus creating an A-Plus experience.

Make sure customers get a realistic perception of how long things take. I heard from a nurse in a hospital of a patient who was sent to the lab for a blood test. The phlebotomist drew the blood sample and took it behind a curtain to be sent off for analysis. As soon as the phlebotomist returned from behind the curtain, , the patient asked what the results of the test were. The lab technician laughed and explained that the test was to be done at another facility and that the results would not be ready until the next day. The point: customers don't always know how long things take. You need to tell them.

Too many businesses fall to the temptation to promise quicker service and hope for the best. They hate to deliver unpleasant news, so they instead offer a time that sounds good but cannot be realistically delivered. In doing so, they miss a significant opportunity to under-promise and over-deliver. It is better to give a realistic time you can beat rather than a pie-in-the-sky estimate you cannot meet.

In addition to regarding people's time, companies need to think about time's cousin: convenience. Offering A-Plus convenience is one of the most powerful ways to build allegiance. This concept is illustrated by two kinds of businesses, pizza and auto lubrication.

The most popular restaurant food in America is pizza. In the late 1950s, when pizza was gaining widespread popularity across the country, it was served just like any other restaurant entrée. People ordered their pizza, waited 15 or 20 minutes for it to bake, and ate it at the restaurant. Then came the convenience pioneers like Domino's. Early in the life of this pizza chain, it made the strategic decision to not have eat-in restaurants and to focus exclusively on take-out (what Europeans call "take away") and on delivery service.

The strategy was a hit. People came to associate Domino's with the 30-minute-delivery guarantee, and in turn Domino's and its competitors taught America a new way of buying restaurant food.

Since then, countless pizza chains and independent restaurants have followed that model. Today, meals prepared outside the home account for nearly half the U.S. food-dollar spending. The Food Marketing Institute says that "Americans want to spend no more than 15 minutes preparing a meal. . . . Today's shoppers want their food and they want it now." Seven out of ten households buy "home meal replacements" (otherwise known as take-out) at least once a month.[3]

Of course, the choices now go far beyond pizza or restaurant meals alone. Supermarkets and delis provide a wide range of prepared meals that need nothing more than heating and eating. Food producers are packaging ingredients together so customers can prepare complete meals without having to buy the ingredients separately. Shredded potatoes, chopped peppers, onions, and diced ham are provided in separate plastic bags within a box describing the meal. Pizza crusts are sold with packets of topping, prepared sandwiches are packaged with chips and a cookie to make an instant box lunch. All these efforts are attempts to meet customer needs for convenience.

Another classic convenience breakthrough is the stand-alone automobile oil-change business, which emerged in the late 1970s and 80s. Before companies like Jiffy Lube, Q-Lube, and Minute Lube, auto owners typically took their cars to dealerships or gas stations to have the oil in their cars changed. They dropped their cars off, caught a ride to work, and then returned after work to pick up their cars. It could easily be an all-day ordeal and was pretty inconvenient. Then a came the quick-lube shop.

Today, we go to a Jiffy Lube or similar shop and have a cup of coffee in a customer lounge while a team of technicians pounces on our car, changes the oil, lubes the grease fittings, checks the tire pressure and all fluid levels, and even vacuums the inside. The whole process takes 10 or 15 minutes. This is A-Plus convenience.

## Make things easier for people

Another way businesses provide A-Plus service is by taking the hassle out of cumbersome systems. Unnecessary paperwork is an area where many companies can improve. Smart companies regularly look at the forms or applications customers and employees need to complete and determine if these are all really necessary. They check for redundancy or requests for unnecessary information that may be making the paperwork process more difficult than it needs to be. Some of the better mortgage or consumer-loan companies streamline the application process by pre-completing parts of the paperwork. For example, a credit union mortgage department I recently worked with downloaded all relevant credit and account information from my account before giving me forms to complete. I needed to fill out only a few lines.

Likewise, a used-auto dealership I bought from had all the information about the car pre-printed on the sales documents. The sales rep slipped a few forms into his computer printer, and the otherwise complicated paperwork was reduced to a matter of a few signatures.

By contrast, I recently had the unpleasant experience of filling out some forms for a healthcare provider. Each form required me to re-enter my name, address, phone number, Social Security number, and such. It got annoying.

Look at your organization to determine if you are requiring repetitive busywork from people. Then A-Plus them by eliminating it.

## Create once-and-done service

"That's not my department," may be one of the least-favorite phrases for customers to hear. When people have to repeatedly tell their story to person after person while seeking a solution, it drives them nuts. Companies can build allegiance by offering once-and-done service. Make it easy for customers and employees to get everything they need and solve any problem at a single place and time.

The Ritz-Carlton Hotels are well known for their simple employee position, that they are "ladies and gentlemen serving ladies and gentlemen." When a hotel guest asks any employee for something, that employee "owns" that request or problem until it is fulfilled or solved. If a guest asks a maid where he can get a copy of a foreign-language newspaper, the maid will either get the paper for him or find out where the guest can get it. The maid is empowered to take the time to run to a newsstand if that will get the guest what he wants. It's once-and-done service, and it blows customers away. This hotel chain won the prestigious Malcolm Baldridge Quality Award in part because of such an exceptional service philosophy.

At the heart of once-and-done service is employee willingness and ability to take responsibility for meeting needs and reducing customer inconvenience. Strong companies hire people with initiative and then empower them to do whatever the customer needs. I'll talk more in Chapter 9 about the importance of empowering and motivating employees.

## Make doing business easy

A *Wall Street Journal* article revealed a "secret weapon" used by discount retailers to "once again trounce traditional department stores." The article explained, "Was it sophisticated pricing, the latest in-store design, or cutting-edge inventory management? Actually, after twenty years of growing discounter dominance, a simpler explanation rolls into view: the shopping cart."

The article goes on to say that the impact of something as simple as a shopping cart is significant. A marketing-research firm found that "the average shopper with a cart buys 7.2 items, while the customer without a cart buys 6.1. As old-fashioned as they seem, carts are perfectly suited for the way people shop today: They're pressed for time and buy more in fewer trips. Mothers struggling to corral children love them. The growing ranks of senior citizens lean on carts for support and appreciate not having to carry their purchases."[4]

Shopping malls are beginning to recognize the importance of making shopping easier. Worried about competition from e-commerce, developers are working to cluster similar stores together so customers can comparison shop.

The traditional mall was designed to be difficult. Retailers wanted to increase exposure to their stores by forcing people to wander through the malls to shop. The more the customer walks, the greater the chance he or she will find something else to buy. But e-commerce is changing this too. People want to compare prices and selection at similar stores, and they don't want to have to walk far to do it. (After all, they can do it very easily online.) Many frustrated, time-pressed shoppers have already defected from malls to big-box discounters (Wal-Mart, K-Mart, Target, Home Depot) where they can get everything they need in one place.[5]

## Offer ancillary services

Loblaw's Supermarkets, Canada's largest chain, offers an ever-growing range of ancillary services to its shoppers. Its latest innovation at a new Toronto store is a complete women-only fitness club that is equipped with saunas, tanning beds, and a daycare center and that offers everything from treadmills to Tae-Bo classes, just steps from the cauliflower. The *Wall Street Journal* reports that, "Like many grocery-store chains, Loblaw rents store space to dry cleaners, liquor stores, coffee shops, and has in-house pharmacies and banking centers. But few chains carry the concept as far as Loblaw does. . . . [T]he chain has started offering video-game and cell-phone sales outlets in some of its stores. In addition it began leasing space to the Club Monoco Inc. clothing store chain and teaching community cooking lessons in stores."[6] Such ancillary services create A-Plus convenience for the chain's customers while providing one-stop shopping for almost every need.

Enlightened companies also earn employee allegiance by offering similar conveniences for their staff personnel. Some of the best companies to work for offer chair massages, recreational outlets, handy refreshments, and even concierge services for their employees.

## Simplify the product

The running joke about people being unable to program a video player indicates the constant need to simplify products for exceptional ease of use and convenience. The computer industry has made quantum leaps with plug-and-play technology, but it still has a ways to go. The newly emerging market for "information appliances" opens new possibilities. Information appliances are simplified computers that buyers can plug in and hook up to the Internet. They don't have the computing power of regular PCs, but most users never need it. They allow users to surf the Net and use email without the complicated processes associated with setting up a typical PC. And, of course, they cost a lot less.

On a more mundane level, product packaging is responding to the customer's desire for convenience. The newest Kellogg cereal, Special-K Plus, is packaged in a re-sealable box that looks like a half-gallon milk carton. It contains the same amount of cereal as larger, more cumbersome boxes but stores in less space and is easy to pour. This joins squeeze bottles of condiments and easy-to-stack containers of various types to offer consumers "little-things" improvements in convenience.

# A Final Thought

Customers and employees are easily surprised by efficient service that goes beyond what they anticipate. Likewise, they appreciate anything that can make life more convenient for them. The need for time-saving, convenient products and services has spun off some pretty innovative timesavers such as drive-in mortuaries, quickie-wedding chapels, and the like. While those examples may carry the principle further than most of us want to go, they do reflect the almost-universal desire for efficient, timely service with a minimum of inconvenience.

Smart companies apply the "little-things" principle. They recognize that little things can make big differences for customers and employees. I saw an example of this during the busy Christmas season when a package-shipping store sent a greeting card to all its customers and included with it a shipping label the customer could fill it out in advance when bringing in packages to ship.

Other little things I appreciate are restaurant servers providing me with my check promptly so that I can leave and refilling my beverage before I even ask. My favorite servers anticipate my needs and meet them promptly. Any business serious about building customer and employee allegiance would be smart to develop a constant flow of fresh ideas for improving convenience and speed of service.

Constantly look for opportunities to exceed what your customer has come to anticipate with regard to speed and convenience.

## Notes

1. Louise Lee, "Online Grocers: Finally Delivering the Lettuce," *Business Week online*, April 28, 2003.

2. Jane Black, "Online Extra: Why Online Grocers Won't All Go Hungry," *Business Week online*, May 14, 2001.

3. Jane Bennett Clarke, "Washed, Cooked and Priced to Go," *Kiplinger's Personal Finance*, January 2000, p. 135.

4. Joseph B. Cahill, "The Secret Weapon of Big Discounters: Lowly Shopping Carts," *Wall Street Journal*, November 24, 1999, p. 1.

5. Calmetta Y. Coleman, "Making Malls (Gasp!) Convenient," *Wall Street Journal*, February 8, 2000, p. B1.

6. Joel A. Baglole, "Loblaw's Supermarkets Add Fitness Clubs to Offerings," *Wall Street Journal*, December 27, 1999, p. B4.

# Actualizing the A-Plus Allegiance Strategy

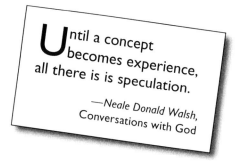

Until a concept becomes experience, all there is is speculation.

—Neale Donald Walsh, Conversations with God

## The Way It Is . . .

Each year *Fortune* magazine publishes an issue featuring the best companies to work for. In the most recent version[1], *Fortune* surveyed a random sample of employees from 269 candidate companies—more than 1,000 firms were considered—to get their opinions about their workplaces, and reported—

A total of 40,713 employees responded to the survey (the "Great Place to Work Trust Index," an instrument created by the Great Place to Work Institute in San Francisco). Nearly half gave us additional written comments. We also asked each of the companies to fill out a questionnaire describing its HR policies and workplace culture. In scoring the responses, we placed the greatest weight on the employee responses (two-thirds of the total), with the remainder being our evaluation of the company's benefits and practices.

The company that ranked No. 1 in 2003 was stockbroker Edward Jones.

One of the critical distinguishing features of all the top companies is their commitment to employee training. According to the Fortune article, Edward Jones "spends 3.8% of its payroll on training, with an average of 146 hours for every employee. New brokers at the 7,781 branches get more than four times that much. Why does Jones invest so much in its people? In order to grow, you have to be trained."

The remarkable success story of JetBlue airline is another example of attention to its people as they strive for excellent customer service. CEO Davis Neeleman makes no apology for focusing all his efforts on building customer allegiance, a strategy that has driven one of the greatest growth stories in recent history.

While other airlines have been cutting back in a declining economy, JetBlue has been buying hundreds of new planes and garnering thousands of converts to its service. In a speech to Northwestern University, Neeleman said little about the financial tactics or operational strategies of JetBlue. His entire lecture centered on the kinds of details that are winning customer and employee allegiance. All employees are called "crew members," customers enjoy roomier leather seats with individual TVs, reservation clerks (oops, crew members) work out of their homes after training to allow them maximum flexibility, and walk-up fares are not inflated for the last-minute traveler. Neeleman himself spends countless hours flying and walking through the aircraft cabin talking with his customers face-to-face and listening to their comments. On the battlefield of commercial aviation, JetBlue is becoming a giant.[2]

Every day, thousands of companies around the world consider ways to improve customer service, strengthen customer and employee relationships, and build allegiance. Managers and leaders seek to evaluate how their organizations are doing and come up with new ideas for reducing customer turnoffs in value, systems, and people. Better leaders also search for ways to A-Plus their customers and employees. They may not use the terminology used in this book, but they wrestle with achieving the same end result.

Management functions inevitably involve *people.* And getting people to do things is like herding cats. Herein lies the universal challenge of management: accomplishing work with and through other people. If managers try to "fly solo" or do it all alone, the likelihood of success drops dramatically. Group involvement at all levels is essential to actualizing an A-Plus strategy.

# Building Allegiance Through Effective Management

Successfully implementing an allegiance strategy calls for creatively applying the critical management functions of *planning, organizing, motivating,* and *controlling.* In this chapter, we will look at these functions as they relate to the creation and actualization of an A-Plus approach to building allegiance. This quick review of management tasks is intended as a reminder, certainly not as new information. Stepping back and taking a back-to-basics look at the process in the context of customer allegiance can be helpful.

## Plan an A-Plus approach

Effective planning includes both big-picture thinking (setting a vision, developing objectives, and gathering the resources needed) and shorter-term implementation activities. Big-picture planning usually involves intensive strategy development, including the articulation of foundation concepts on which the company's overall efforts will be based.

The manager's daily planning actions should look ahead to what must be done to maintain and improve performance, to solve problems, and to develop employee competence. When planning, a manager sets objectives in performance areas—tasks that are to be pursued this week, this month, and this year. Having set these objectives, the manager then thinks through such questions as these:

- What specific tasks are to be done to reach these objectives?
- Who will carry out these tasks?
- When will these tasks take place?
- Where will this work be done?
- What resources will be needed?

Such planning should be based on information received from customers, organization members, and other stakeholders. Throughout this book, I have shown you ways to gather perceptions and hard data from and about customers and employees. Use such data in the planning process by—

- Consistently, persistently, gathering good-quality information and
- Using the information to implement and adjust an ongoing approach using the tactics discussed in this book.

### Articulate a vision

As part of the planning function, management should articulate a vision for customer and employee relationships. But—and this is very important—vision statements *should be developed as a group process.* Vision or mission statements proclaimed by managers without input from others are seen as fiats and have less power to influence individual behavior than do statements developed with the participation of the people responsible for making the vision a reality. People buy into what they have helped create.

If your company has no such mission statement, has not articulated a vision in a concise and memorable form, or if the statement has gotten stale, work with your people to articulate a fresh theme or credo—a customer and employee allegiance mission statement.

As I consult with organizations, I typically ask if they have such a theme or mission statement. Fairly often I get answers something like this: "Oh, yes, we have 13 points to excellent service." My reply to that is, "Oh, really? What's point 11?"

The response to that is usually, "Well, I don't know exactly." Then I'd ask, "How about point 6? Which one is that?" As you can imagine, the typical answer is something like, "I'm not sure. I actually haven't *memorized* all the points, but we have this statement posted throughout the company."

Unfortunately, simply posting a list of principles does little good. To articulate a useful theme, organization members need to come up with a succinct, clear statement of what the organization is about and how it could be seen as unique. Someone once said that a good mission statement is one that you could repeat at gunpoint! Such a statement provides something that all employees can remember and buy into as a guiding statement that will shape their actions and help them make decisions.

Let's look at a couple of examples.

- Federal Express expresses its theme in three words: "Absolutely, positively, overnight." They will get packages delivered absolutely, positively, overnight, and they're 99.8 percent successful at doing that.

- The direct-marketing clothier Lands' End has a simple motto or credo that has just two words: "Guaranteed. Period." This communicates the company's highest service priority.

- Wal-Mart pledges "to provide a range of products that deliver value to Middle America."

- A small bookbindery states that it will "guide customers through the entire publishing maze."[3]

- A credit union's theme is simply "people helping people" [with their financial needs].

A *Harvard Business Review*[4] article told of a Seattle restaurant staff who wrestled with this idea of a simple, clear theme. After carefully looking at the company through the eyes of their customers and determining just what their restaurant guests want from them, they came up with this theme: "Your enjoyment guaranteed. Always." That is exactly what they offer their guests—enjoyment.

The employees made the theme into an acronym: YEGA. While YEGA may not mean anything to most of us, it became a catchphrase for their organization. They developed YEGA promotions and YEGA bucks and YEGA pins and hats to get employees involved in the spirit of YEGA. It was fun, it was interesting, and it constantly reminded employees of that simple four-word theme: "Your enjoyment guaranteed. Always."

To fulfill the management responsibility of articulating an effective allegiance-building theme, try these important steps:

- **Commit to work on the process** of identifying a theme that is *succinct, clear, and descriptive* of your organization's uniqueness.

- **Gather ideas from customers.** Ask them, "What five things do you as customers want as you do business with us?" Ask them to respond quickly off the top of their heads, and look carefully at the language they use.

- **Get employees together** and ask what they most want from their company and what they think customers want. Ask them to respond quickly, and write down their responses so you can carefully examine the language they used in responding. As you gather perceptions from both customers and employees, you'll notice that some terms come up repeatedly. These often-repeated terms are good words to put into your customer- and employee-allegiance theme. In drafting a theme, remember that participation and input from customers and employees is very important. If your company uses the Allegiance Technologies Active Listening System, you will have verbatim recorded comments that can provide excellent data for you to work with.

- **Write several rough drafts** of the theme; don't be too quick to come up with the finished version. Phrase the final version in ten or fewer words, if possible.

- **Make the theme into an acronym** for ease of recall, if possible. The YEGA example given earlier is an example of such an acronym.

Once your organization's theme is articulated, be sure it is communicated *often*. Make it a regular part of any company communication efforts. Print it on your organization's letterhead and include it in your Web site; repeat it regularly at company meetings; tell your customers what it is. In short, be redundant and reinforce it to anyone who will listen.

A simple way to determine whether your people are buying in to the vision is to spontaneously talk to some of your employees and ask them to describe the organization's theme. Especially invite an employee who has been with the organization for ten days or less to identify the theme. If he or she can't do it, make the theme a more prominent part of your new-employee orientation. (But go easy on the new kid. He'll remember it next time.)

What good does it do just to be able to repeat such a phrase? The answer is that it's a start. Repeating some words may seem meaningless at first, but eventually the sense of the statement will sink in and people will adjust their behaviors to act congruently with the vision. Most organizations fall far short even of that level of agreement. Focusing people on a common theme can be well worth the effort.

One final note: A theme is not necessarily forever. As an organization changes directions or as markets or economic conditions change, a theme may be modified. Some organizations may want to use a theme statement for a limited period of time, much the way advertisers use an ad slogan for only a few years. Modifying the theme should not, however, be done without careful thought. Consistency of direction is usually an asset.

### Set objectives for your allegiance strategy

Another planning function involves determining desired service results and deciding how and when to achieve service goals. Target the kinds of improvements that are measurable and reasonable. Of course, in order to measure change, you need a starting point.

### Establish benchmarks: "How are we doing?"

Each organization will have its own effectiveness measures, but one that can be used by anyone is the three-question "Customer Allegiance Index," which is derived from asking customers (or employees) the three questions you read about in Chapter 1:

1. Overall, how satisfied were you with [name of company, department, or organization]?

2. How likely would you be to recommend [name of company, department, or organization] to a friend or associate?

3. How likely are you to do business with [name of company, department, or organization] when future needs arise?

### Be patient about change

Don't expect Customer Allegiance Index results to change overnight. Changing human behavior takes time, and the organizational results may not show up right away. Don't become frustrated (or get after your people) if the scores change slowly.

Use measures to set goals, establish priorities, and determine the sequence and timing of tactic implementation. You can't fix everything at once, so look for the kinds of results that can give you the most impact for the effort involved—pick the low-hanging fruit first. Handling the obvious shortcomings that reflect value, systems, and people turnoffs can motivate your people to tackle the more difficult problems later.

Budget for improvements. Many changes, especially those that attack systems or value turnoffs, require the expenditure of money or other resources. Once better methods are developed, establish them as policy—as standing decisions on how the organization is to work so that you need not re-visit the decision. For example, you may decide that the staff of customer-contact people will automatically be increased each time the number of customers served or the customer waiting time reaches a certain level.

### Consider the use of consultants

At the risk of sounding self-serving, I recommend that you consider retaining a qualified consultant as you plan and implement an employee- and customer-allegiance strategy. A qualified consultant can take a detached, global view. He or she can peruse the forest without getting too tangled in the trees. Ideas and applications the consultant has used with other client organizations can be brought to your organization, and the strategy launch can happen without taking managers away from other duties.

With my clients, I describe a process that outlines their responsibilities and mine. The guidelines are clear, and the process moves forward systematically when a conscientious consultant applies his or her expertise to the important tasks involved in developing and actualizing an organization's allegiance strategy.

## Organize and staff for building allegiance

The management task of organizing involves arranging the work sequence and assigning areas of responsibility and authority. Having set the theme, determined benchmarks, set some goals, and identified activities of the various work units, managers must then take these two steps:

- Assign responsibilities to specific employees or work groups, and

- Give employees the supporting authority to fulfill their responsibilities (empowerment).

## Organize people and delineate authority

The organizing function involves such actions as clarifying the organizational structure (who reports to whom, what functions or departments coordinate with each other, and so on) assigning certain responsibilities, and giving authority to employees. People at all levels need to know the scope and range of their jobs—including what they can or cannot do for the customer.

Among companies known for giving legendary service, people at all levels are given a lot of latitude. Nordstrom employees, for example, know they can do almost anything to meet a customer's needs. They have been known to send clothing to customers using overnight delivery (regardless of the additional cost) and to give customers gifts or additional merchandise to recompense for any customer disappointment. Ritz Carlton hotel employees are encouraged to take personal ownership of any problem a guest may have, guided solely by their theme of "ladies and gentlemen serving ladies and gentlemen." If a guest's need comes to an employee's attention, that employee is fully empowered to drop what he or she is doing and serve that customer's needs. Bellhops have been known to rush out of the hotel to buy a foreign newspaper for a guest who was disappointed that the publication wasn't available in the hotel's gift shop. Managers have given employees at all levels the authority to do whatever it takes, no questions asked.

By contrast, an auto dealership I once did business with used its commitment to a no-dicker, fixed-price selling policy to strictly limit employee discretion. A salesperson there would be fired for giving customers a free set of floor mats, for example. Even if sales reps bought such customer bonuses as floor mats with their own money, they would be reprimanded and perhaps fired for doing so. Limiting employee discretion is not the way to build employee or customer allegiance. It defeats everything that an A-Plus strategy stands for and virtually destroys all opportunity for building allegiance. By the way, the auto dealership failed after just a few years of business.

## Staff with quality employees

Managers are responsible for recruiting qualified people for each employee position, for orienting new employees to the company's service expectations, and for training people so that they become proficient by instruction and practice.

Some successful managers recruit by "stealing" good employees from other companies. (That's stated a bit strongly, but the principle works.) As managers encounter people with great attitudes and excellent customer-service skills at other organizations, they might try to hire them away or at least recommend them to company recruiters.

One owner of a chain of fast-food restaurants solved his problem of getting quality employees in a high-turnover industry by giving his business card to employees in other companies who give him good service. He'd say something like, "Thank you for your great service. You did a nice job. If you are ever interested in changing jobs, I'd appreciate your calling me personally. I'm sure I could find a place for you in my organization."

Keep a file of people you'd like to have working for you, and when an opening occurs, contact them. Don't worry if they are working in a totally different type of business. The specifics of your organization can be taught. Great attitudes cannot be.

## Hire people with emotional intelligence

A key characteristic of effective customer-contact people is *emotional intelligence*. A person's "emotional quotient" (EQ) refers to an assortment of non-cognitive skills, capabilities, and competencies that influence a person's ability to succeed in coping with environmental demands and pressures—especially other people. People with high EQ have developed these attributes:

- **Self-awareness**—the ability to know what they are feeling.
- **Self-management** skills—the ability to manage their own emotions and impulses.
- **Self-motivation**—the ability to persist in the face of setbacks and failures.
- **Empathy**—the ability to sense how others are feeling.
- **Social skills**—the ability to handle the emotions of others.

Research into emotional intelligence suggests that employers should consider it in employee selection, especially for jobs that demand a high degree of social interaction.[5] If you are interested in understanding EQ better, you may want to read Daniel Goleman's book, *Working with Emotional Intelligence* (Bantam, 1998).

## Be sure your people have everything they need

Once you have recruited good people, be certain that they have everything they need to do a great job. Be sure that everyone who needs to can find these essential resources:

- a telephone located where it can be heard
- a computer with customer records
- a fax machine, messenger service, or supplies for overnight shipping
- letterhead, envelopes, and postage
- business cards (maybe even the new electronic cards that are played in a CD-ROM drive of a computer)
- product information, pricing schedules, and publications
- policy statements and a printed copy of the company's vision statement

- a desk, writing table, or private place to confer with customers
- office supplies
- a mobile or portable phone

These resource requirements will differ across organizations, but today's customer-allegiance efforts require today's equipment.

### Create growth opportunities for employees

Managers need to be sure that once people are hired, they have ample opportunity to develop their knowledge, attitudes, and skills. The best jobs are those that allow people to grow.

Provide employees with ample training and frequent opportunities to develop their skills. Use the many media available to provide training, including classes, seminars, videotape programs, online courses and other distance-learning programs, and the like.

## Motivate and lead

The management function of motivating and leading is the engine that enables the organization to achieve its objectives. Such leadership includes the following activities:

- **Showing the direction** in which subordinates must go and modeling the appropriate behaviors.
- **Generating the energy** (motivation) that subordinates must feel.
- **Providing the resources** needed to accomplish the tasks.

An organization's leaders set the tone for motivation throughout the organization. Motivation can be simply defined as *providing motives for action*. Leaders provide motives or reasons people should act in particular ways. They also motivate by persuading and inspiring people to take desired action. And, of course, the best leaders motivate by example, not by edict.

## Lead the company's efforts

Managers fulfill their leadership functions by directing and delegating—assigning responsibility and accountability for service results to the people they manage. Other directing functions include coordinating desired efforts in the most efficient combination, managing differences, resolving conflicts, and stimulating creativity and innovation in achieving service goals.

Gaining employee participation can make directing go much easier. People who willingly volunteer to be responsible for some functions are more likely to be committed to these functions than people who are just assigned tasks. Invite people to take charge of portions of your allegiance-building efforts. For example, rotate the responsibility for gathering and reporting on service measures. Let different people see, firsthand, the kinds of feedback you are getting from the Active Listening System™ and invite them to take charge of efforts to remedy specific problems.

## Adjust or modify the reward system

Many companies fall into the trap of rewarding one kind of behavior while hoping employees will produce different behaviors. A commonplace example is the practice of paying people by the hour. What behavior does hourly payment encourage? Taking up hours! Is that what you want your people to do?

A clothing store encouraged employees to work together to meet customer needs, but it set up an incentive program that paid the top individual salesperson a substantial cash award. Did the store get employees working together to meet customer needs? Nope—it got salespeople climbing all over each other to get to the customer before the other guy did.

Think about the behaviors you really want to see in your organization. Then reward those behaviors, not something else. Also, think carefully about whether you want to provide group or individual rewards. Much of customer service is a team effort, so you may want to consider creative use of group rewards.

One client organization I worked with for several years created what it called the Excel program. Employees throughout the organization were awarded Excel points for such things as:

- Receiving an unsolicited compliment from a customer
- Being recognized by their department manager for exceptional service effort or problem handling
- Being "caught" doing something exceptionally well by other organization managers
- Reading the company's service newsletter and completing a brief quiz in the publication
- Attending optional training sessions or classes

Employees earned a certain number of points for each of these actions. At the end of each month, the employee from each department with the most points was selected to attend the "Excel-abration," where a luncheon was served and participants played games for prizes. The prizes were modest (things like dinner certificates, movie passes, small appliances, and tools), but the comradeship was strong and people felt good about the attention they received.

At the end of the year, the company held a bigger Excel-abration. The top point winners from each department for the entire year were invited, along with a guest, to a beautiful dinner and more contests. This time the prizes were more substantial: TVs, exercise equipment, stereos, mountain bikes, and vacation packages.

The Excel program generated a lot of interest and helped sustain ongoing motivation by rewarding the right behaviors.

## Control and evaluate

The final basic management function involves comparing actual results to expected or planned-for results in an effort to identify any deviation from plan. Typically, any deviation from plan calls for adjusting motivation attempts, re-planning of activities to close the gap, allocating resources to meet organizational conditions, or changing the objectives to be more realistic.

Customer allegiance is a critical organizational goal and should be one of the most closely watched indicators of success. This book has suggested a number of ways to assess how you are doing, some more formal than others. Benchmarking is critical to measure changes. But some simple, informal assessments can also provide a good feel for how the company is doing. One simple method is to simply ask a lot of questions.

Author Bill Maynard[6] agrees that the art of management often involves asking lots of questions. He recommends that as managers interact with employees and customers, they ask questions like these:

- What made you mad today?
- What was too complicated?
- What took too long?
- What was just plain silly?
- What caused complaints today?
- What job involved too many people?
- What was misunderstood today?
- What job involved too many actions?
- What costs too much?
- What was wasted?

Commit these questions to memory, and ask them often. Then act (to the degree possible) on the answers people give.

## Harvesting A-Plus Ideas

In addition to the four important management tasks we've just discussed, perhaps the most important step to actualizing an allegiance strategy is to *systematically harvest an ongoing flow of A-Plus ideas* that can make your organization consistently stronger in attracting and keeping customers.

Every employee and every customer should have access to a forum where he or she can offer A-Plus ideas. Employees should also have a forum for participation in deciding which of those harvested ideas to implement.

Set aside some specific A-Plus idea-generating time. Initially, managers may want to use an off-site retreat or specially designated launch meeting. But once an A-Plus approach is up and running, managers should consistently designate additional times to gather ideas. Many of my clients use a few minutes as part of regularly scheduled meetings dedicated to one tactic (say, *convenience* or *value* ideas), or even a sub-portion of a tactic (like *speed of service* or *add-ons*). That may be all that is needed to ensure a constant flow of ideas.

People at all organizational levels can and will provide great A-Plus ideas. I worked, for example, with a hospital client that did a great job of getting employee involvement. As a part of their regular staff meetings, department supervisors designated some time to brainstorm possible A-Plus ideas. To make the process more manageable, they would focus on one opportunity area at a time.

The housekeeping department (janitors and maids) at this hospital came up with an interesting A-Plus idea that illustrates the potential of this strategy. Although at the lower level of the organizational chart, these people were fully empowered to participate. One meeting produced the idea to change the paintings hanging on the walls of the hospital corridors periodically so that patients, especially long-term patients, would have something different to look at—a little thing, but to the elderly and other long-term patients, who could come out of a room for perhaps only a few minutes each day, it was a thoughtful gesture.

The payoff came one day when a housekeeping employee was mopping the hallway and an older lady came out of her room and was admiring a painting. She commented how lovely the painting was, and the janitor put down his mop, came over to the lady, and said, "Ma'am, we change the pictures every week so that you'll have something different to look at." The patient was deeply touched by this gesture of kindness.

This example illustrates several themes discussed throughout this book:

- Little things can have considerable impact.

- Employees at all levels of an organization have good ideas.

- Given the opportunity to share their ideas, employees can and will build greater allegiance for themselves and customers.

## Use brainstorming when creative ideas are needed

The term *brainstorming* has become synonymous with any kind of creative thinking. But that misuses the concept. Brainstorming is a specific technique using explicit rules for idea generation and development. This approach requires a communication climate in which free expression of all kinds of ideas is valued and encouraged—no matter how offbeat or bizarre they may seem. Brainstorming has four basic rules:

1. *Do not criticize any ideas.* No comments; no grunts or groans; no thumbs-down gestures. Just let it come out and be recorded. Never disqualify an idea as being too wild.

2. *Generate the maximum quantity* (initially, don't worry about quality). Try to record as many ideas as possible, without regard to whether they make any sense at this point.

3. *Seize opportunities to "hitchhike"*—to add to or amplify on ideas suggested by others.

Of course, simply stating these rules is much easier than actually following them. Unless great care is taken, nonverbal cues can be interpreted as judgment of ideas—judgment that can discourage additional creative or wild ideas. Avoid that. When using brainstorming, participants should prominently post the rules as a constant reminder.

The climate set by the meeting leader can promote or hamper the use of brainstorming. A climate that encourages humor and informality will work best. So go into a rubber room and have some fun. The nuttiest ideas can sometimes be refined into something workable and ingenious.

## Use a nominal group process when appropriate

Another approach useful in harvesting ideas is the Nominal Group Process (NGP). This is an idea-generating approach that is particularly useful when dealing with potentially emotional, unusually creative, or controversial ideas. Rather than having group members immediately speak up with their point of view (a process that may *commit* them to that view, since they've voiced it publicly), NGP participants write their ideas, privately. Following a clear definition of the problem or issues, group members spend 10 to 20 minutes writing ideas about possible solutions. They then meet and each participant reads one idea from his or her list, which is written on a flip chart in full view of the group. Ideas are recorded but not discussed at this point. This round-robin listing of ideas continues until the members have no further ideas. People may then clarify or amplify an idea. Then participants silently vote on a rank order for the ideas. The steps of the process, once again, are:

1. Silent generation of solution ideas in writing.

2. Round-robin recording of ideas.

3. Discussion of ideas for clarification.

4. Silent voting to rank items (several votes may be needed before a final solution is accepted).

Use brainstorming and NGP to gather ideas from all organization members. Make the harvesting process ongoing. In doing so, you consistently raise the level of expectations and further distinguish your company's unique approach to customer allegiance.

# Summary: Seven Tasks to Initiate and Sustain an A-Plus Customer- and Employee-Allegiance Strategy

Managers can turn good intentions into a workable A-Plus approach based on seven key tasks described briefly below. These tasks do not have to be done in the order presented; several may be done concurrently.

## Task No. 1:
## Orient all employees

Take steps to ensure that all employees clearly understand the need for cultivating customer allegiance. Teach them about the cost of lost customers, how lost customers lead to lost jobs, why poor service givers pay a psychological price, and why developing customer-service professionalism is in their best interest. This step can best be done by conducting a series of training sessions and by providing all organization members with copies of this book and the accompanying workshop handout materials. (Quantity discounts are available.)

Orienting employees in this way gets them all speaking the same language, singing from the same sheet music, pulling in the same direction (whichever metaphor you prefer).

## Task No. 2:
## Build momentum

Conduct regular departmental follow-up meetings after the initial training. Teach basic creativity and group problem-solving skills, and schedule and conduct regular brainstorming sessions to discuss new A-Plus ideas. Show individuals and work groups how to set departmental or team goals.

Construct or modify the reward system so that the most useful activities get the best rewards. Create a reward committee to determine special bonuses, determine budget, and define criteria whereby people can win the rewards. Then develop data-gathering forms or processes that give credit for good works. Distribute "Attaboy" and "Attagirl" cards or small rewards to recognize success immediately.

## Task No. 3:
## Monitor customer expectations and employee behavior

Teach naive listening techniques to employees and managing-by-questions approaches to supervisors. Recognize the value of customers as sources of improvement ideas. Install and learn from the Active Listening System input. Schedule focus groups regularly. Record, digest, and keep data and trends analyses. Discuss these in regular staff meetings.

Depending on the nature of your business, conduct regular shopper surveys to determine the kinds of service people are getting from employees. These surveys should typically be done by independent shopper services that provide immediate and specific feedback to employees.

## Task No. 4:
## Establish systematic customer-retention and follow-up efforts

Develop creative customer-follow-up techniques. Schedule regular follow-up with mail-outs, email contacts, announcements, and special incentives. Try such other allegiance builders as customer photos or customer letters posted on display. Acknowledge "Customer of the Month" and "Employee of the Month" recognition, or something similar.

## Task No. 5:
## Provide continuation training for employees

Schedule repeat basic training for new employees. Also schedule regular continuation training where employees can receive instruction on such tasks as writing customer correspondence, handling difficult people, improving telephone techniques, and mastering time and task management.

## Task No. 6:
## Conduct ongoing systems reviews

Create task forces to review systems. Employ explorer groups to visit competitors or similar businesses that have good ideas. Energize your suggestion program (using the Allegiance Technologies Employee Active Listening System) to improve systems by announcing and publicizing the suggestion program, budgeting award money, and forming a review committee to evaluate suggestions submitted.

## Task No. 7:
## Recruit, develop, and retain excellent employees

Attract and select exceptional service personnel by developing aptitude and attitude testing and interviewing procedures. Proactively invite promising employees from other businesses to join you.

When new employees are hired, be sure to clarify promotion criteria and tie these criteria to the customer-service reward system. In short, base employee advancement on service attitudes and skills. As part of this process, be sure to conduct meaningful performance reviews with service criteria being measured and factored into the reviews.

# A Final Thought

*The ideas in this book will do you no good.*

Until you put them into practice. Companies can talk about customer allegiance until they are blue in the face, but until they apply the kinds of tactics described in this book, nothing much is likely to happen. If they keep doing what they've always done, they'll keep getting the results they've always gotten.

I hope you are motivated to try some of the approaches described in these nine chapters. I have intentionally kept the book concise, hoping that you will read and re-read these ideas many times and, more important, that you will implement them.

Try the seven tasks you've just read about, and see what happens. With them, you have at your disposal a proven process for translating good intentions into a realistic, workable strategy for building unprecedented levels of employee and customer allegiance.

As the famous footwear ads so succinctly put it—JUST DO IT.

## Notes

1. Robert Levering and Milton Moskowitz, "How We Pick the 100 Best," *Fortune*, January 7, 2003.

2. David Neeleman's lecture to Northwestern University's prestigious Kellogg School of Management was delivered on April 6, 2003, and covered by C-Span.

3. Tracey Lowrance, "Customer Service Mission Statement: The Key to Fulfilling Customer Needs," online at www.Digital-Women.com (a site for how-to business articles for women), accessed August 19, 2003.

4. See Firnstahl, T. W., "My Employees Are My Service Guarantee," *Harvard Business Review,* July-August 1989, pp. 28-32.

5. This description of emotional intelligence is adapted from Steven P. Robbins, *Essentials of Organizational Behavior,* 7th ed. (Upper Saddle River, NJ: Prentice-Hall, Inc., 2002), pp. 40-41. The concept of IE was first developed by Daniel Goleman in his book, *Emotional Intelligence* (New York: Bantam, 1995).

6. B. Maynard, "How to Manage with Questions," in *TeleProfessional,* 209 W. 5th Street, Waterloo, IA 50701-5420.

# Application Guide for Building Customer and Employee Allegiance

## A-Plus Worksheets

These worksheets will be useful to you and your organization as you implement a customer-allegiance strategy.

This appendix is an abbreviated version of a longer workbook used in association with training and consulting sessions conducted by the author.

You are welcome and encouraged to copy and use these worksheets as needed.

# Worksheets

*A-Plus Worksheets © 2004 Paul R. Timm. May be copied as needed for organizational use.*

# Packaging Ideas

Use this form to generate possible A-Plus packaging ideas as discussed in Chapter 5, "Giving A-Plus Value."

Working alone or with a small group, jot down as many ideas as possible about packaging goods and services without regard for whether they are practical or immediately usable. Then review all ideas for possible adoption in your organization. Put a check mark next to the ones you want to try.

❑ _____

❑ _____

❑ _____

❑ _____

❑ _____

❑ _____

❑ _____

❑ _____

❑ _____

❑ _____

❑ _____

❑ _____

❑ _____

❑ _____

❑ _____

❑ _____

❑ _____

❑ _____

Develop a priority list indicating when you will apply each selected idea. Describe tasks necessary to enact the A-Plus ideas (what is needed, who will initiate, etc.).

# Guarantee, Agreement, and Warranty Ideas

Use this form to generate possible A-Plus ideas about guarantees, agreements, and warranties your organization could offer customers and employees.

Working alone or with a small group, jot down as many ideas as possible without regard for whether they are practical or immediately usable. Then review all ideas for possible adoption in your organization. Put a check mark next to the ones you want to try.

❑ _____

❑ _____

❑ _____

❑ _____

❑ _____

❑ _____

❑ _____

❑ _____

❑ _____

❑ _____

❑ _____

❑ _____

❑ _____

❑ _____

❑ _____

❑ _____

❑ _____

Develop a priority list indicating when you will apply each selected idea. Describe tasks necessary to enact the A-Plus ideas (what is needed, who will initiate, etc.).

# Goodness-of-Fit Ideas

Use this form to generate possible A-Plus ideas about improving goodness of fit between your products and customer and employee needs.

Working alone or with a small group, jot down as many ideas as possible without regard for whether they are practical or immediately usable. Then review all ideas for possible adoption in your organization. Put a check mark next to the ones you want to try.

❑ _____

❑ _____

❑ _____

❑ _____

❑ _____

❑ _____

❑ _____

❑ _____

❑ _____

❑ _____

❑ _____

❑ _____

❑ _____

❑ _____

❑ _____

❑ _____

❑ _____

Develop a priority list indicating when you will apply each selected idea. Describe tasks necessary to enact the A-Plus ideas (what is needed, who will initiate, etc.).

# Memorable-Experiences Ideas

Use this form to generate possible A-Plus ideas for making customer and employee experiences with you more memorable (as discussed in Chapter 5).

Working alone or with a small group, jot down as many ideas as possible without regard for whether they are practical or immediately usable. Then review all ideas for possible adoption in your organization. Put a check mark next to the ones you want to try.

❑ _____

❑ _____

❑ _____

❑ _____

❑ _____

❑ _____

❑ _____

❑ _____

❑ _____

❑ _____

❑ _____

❑ _____

❑ _____

❑ _____

❑ _____

❑ _____

❑ _____

❑ _____

Develop a priority list indicating when you will apply each selected idea. Describe tasks necessary to enact the A-Plus ideas (what is needed, who will initiate, etc.).

# Unique and Shared Values Ideas

Use this form to generate possible A-Plus ideas for demonstrating to customers and employees your shared values.

Working alone or with a small group, jot down as many ideas as possible without regard for whether they are practical or immediately usable. Then review all ideas for possible adoption in your organization. Put a check mark next to the ones you want to try.

❑ _____

❑ _____

❑ _____

❑ _____

❑ _____

❑ _____

❑ _____

❑ _____

❑ _____

❑ _____

❑ _____

❑ _____

❑ _____

❑ _____

❑ _____

❑ _____

❑ _____

Develop a priority list indicating when you will apply each selected idea. Describe tasks necessary to enact the A-Plus ideas (what is needed, who will initiate, etc.).

# Credibility-Enhancement Ideas

Use this form to generate possible A-Plus ideas for projecting enhanced credibility to your customers and employees.

Working alone or with a small group, jot down as many ideas as possible without regard for whether they are practical or immediately usable. Then review all ideas for possible adoption in your organization. Put a check mark next to the ones you want to try.

❑ _____

❑ _____

❑ _____

❑ _____

❑ _____

❑ _____

❑ _____

❑ _____

❑ _____

❑ _____

❑ _____

❑ _____

❑ _____

❑ _____

❑ _____

❑ _____

❑ _____

❑ _____

Develop a priority list indicating when you will apply each selected idea. Describe tasks necessary to enact the A-Plus ideas (what is needed, who will initiate, etc.).

# Add-on Ideas

Use this form to generate possible A-Plus ideas using add-ons. What kinds of things can you give away (or sell) that will make your core products more valuable to customers? What kinds of add-ons might pleasantly surprise employees?

Working alone or with a small group, jot down as many ideas as possible without regard for whether they are practical or immediately usable. Then review all ideas for possible adoption in your organization. Put a check mark next to the ones you want to try.

❑ _____

❑ _____

❑ _____

❑ _____

❑ _____

❑ _____

❑ _____

❑ _____

❑ _____

❑ _____

❑ _____

❑ _____

❑ _____

❑ _____

❑ _____

❑ _____

❑ _____

Develop a priority list indicating when you will apply each selected idea. Describe tasks necessary to enact the A-Plus ideas (what is needed, who will initiate, etc.).

# Handholding Ideas

Use this form to generate possible A-Plus information ideas. How can your organization better provide customer or employee handholding as discussed in Chapter 6?

Working alone or with a small group, jot down as many ideas as possible without regard for whether they are practical or immediately usable. Then review all ideas for possible adoption in your organization. Put a check mark next to the ones you want to try.

❑ _____

❑ _____

❑ _____

❑ _____

❑ _____

❑ _____

❑ _____

❑ _____

❑ _____

❑ _____

❑ _____

❑ _____

❑ _____

❑ _____

❑ _____

❑ _____

❑ _____

Develop a priority list indicating when you will apply each selected idea. Describe tasks necessary to enact the A-Plus ideas (what is needed, who will initiate, etc.).

*A-Plus Worksheets © 2004 Paul R. Timm. May be copied as needed for organizational use.*

# Media-Use Ideas

Use this form to generate possible A-Plus information ideas as discussed in Chapter 6. How can your organization better use various communication media to provide better customer information?

Working alone or with a small group, jot down as many ideas as possible without regard for whether they are practical or immediately usable. Then review all ideas for possible adoption in your organization. Put a check mark next to the ones you want to try.

❑ _____

❑ _____

❑ _____

❑ _____

❑ _____

❑ _____

❑ _____

❑ _____

❑ _____

❑ _____

❑ _____

❑ _____

❑ _____

❑ _____

❑ _____

❑ _____

Develop a priority list indicating when you will apply each selected idea. Describe tasks necessary to enact the A-Plus ideas (what is needed, who will initiate, etc.).

# Message-Clarity Ideas

Use this form to generate possible A-Plus information ideas as discussed in Chapter 6. How can your organization improve message clarity on materials you are currently using to provide better customer information? Consider the use of different layouts, icons, or graphics, as well as improved wording.

Working alone or with a small group, jot down as many ideas as possible without regard for whether they are practical or immediately usable. Then review all ideas for possible adoption in your organization. Put a check mark next to the ones you want to try.

❑ _____

❑ _____

❑ _____

❑ _____

❑ _____

❑ _____

❑ _____

❑ _____

❑ _____

❑ _____

❑ _____

❑ _____

❑ _____

❑ _____

❑ _____

❑ _____

❑ _____

Develop a priority list indicating when you will apply each selected idea. Describe tasks necessary to enact the A-Plus ideas (what is needed, who will initiate, etc.).

# User Groups or Classes

Use this form to generate possible A-Plus information ideas on how your organization might initiate user groups or classes to provide customers with better information.

Working alone or with a small group, jot down as many ideas as possible without regard for whether they are practical or immediately usable. Then review all ideas for possible adoption in your organization. Put a check mark next to the ones you want to try.

❑ _____

❑ _____

❑ _____

❑ _____

❑ _____

❑ _____

❑ _____

❑ _____

❑ _____

❑ _____

❑ _____

❑ _____

❑ _____

❑ _____

❑ _____

❑ _____

❑ _____

Develop a priority list indicating when you will apply each selected idea. Describe tasks necessary to enact the A-Plus ideas (what is needed, who will initiate, etc.).

# Treating Customers Like Guests

Use this form to generate possible A-Plus ideas for treating customers and employees like guests when they initially come into your business, department, or organization.

Working alone or with a small group, jot down as many ideas as possible without regard for whether they are practical or immediately usable. Then review all ideas for possible adoption in your organization. Put a check mark next to the ones you want to try.

❑ _____

❑ _____

❑ _____

❑ _____

❑ _____

❑ _____

❑ _____

❑ _____

❑ _____

❑ _____

❑ _____

❑ _____

❑ _____

❑ _____

❑ _____

❑ _____

❑ _____

Develop a priority list indicating when you will apply each selected idea. Describe tasks necessary to enact the A-Plus ideas (what is needed, who will initiate, etc.).

# Developing Rapport

Use this form to generate possible A-Plus ideas for developing rapport with customers and employees.

Working alone or with a small group, jot down as many ideas as possible without regard for whether they are practical or immediately usable. Then review all ideas for possible adoption in your organization. Put a check mark next to the ones you want to try.

❑ _____

❑ _____

❑ _____

❑ _____

❑ _____

❑ _____

❑ _____

❑ _____

❑ _____

❑ _____

❑ _____

❑ _____

❑ _____

❑ _____

❑ _____

❑ _____

❑ _____

Develop a priority list indicating when you will apply each selected idea. Describe tasks necessary to enact the A-Plus ideas (what is needed, who will initiate, etc.).

# Creating a Communication Circle

Use this form to generate possible A-Plus ideas for creating a communication circle with customers and employees (as discussed in Chapter 7).

Working alone or with a small group, jot down as many ideas as possible without regard for whether they are practical or immediately usable. Then review all ideas for possible adoption in your organization. Put a check mark next to the ones you want to try.

❑ _____

❑ _____

❑ _____

❑ _____

❑ _____

❑ _____

❑ _____

❑ _____

❑ _____

❑ _____

❑ _____

❑ _____

❑ _____

❑ _____

❑ _____

❑ _____

Develop a priority list indicating when you will apply each selected idea. Describe tasks necessary to enact the A-Plus ideas (what is needed, who will initiate, etc.).

# Better Telephone Techniques

Use this form to generate possible A-Plus ideas for using the telephone more effectively when interacting with customers and employees.

Working alone or with a small group, jot down as many ideas as possible without regard for whether they are practical or immediately usable. Then review all ideas for possible adoption in your organization. Put a check mark next to the ones you want to try.

❑ _____

❑ _____

❑ _____

❑ _____

❑ _____

❑ _____

❑ _____

❑ _____

❑ _____

❑ _____

❑ _____

❑ _____

❑ _____

❑ _____

❑ _____

❑ _____

❑ _____

Develop a priority list indicating when you will apply each selected idea. Describe tasks necessary to enact the A-Plus ideas (what is needed, who will initiate, etc.).

# Enjoying Association with Customers

Use this form to generate possible A-Plus ideas for enjoying work with your customers and employees.

Working alone or with a small group, jot down as many ideas as possible without regard for whether they are practical or immediately usable. Then review all ideas for possible adoption in your organization. Put a check mark next to the ones you want to try.

❑ _____

❑ _____

❑ _____

❑ _____

❑ _____

❑ _____

❑ _____

❑ _____

❑ _____

❑ _____

❑ _____

❑ _____

❑ _____

❑ _____

❑ _____

❑ _____

❑ _____

Develop a priority list indicating when you will apply each selected idea. Describe tasks necessary to enact the A-Plus ideas (what is needed, who will initiate, etc.).

# Attention to Customer Timing

Review the material in Chapter 8, "Giving A-Plus Convenience," before completing this worksheet. Then use this form to generate possible A-Plus convenience ideas. How might your organization better provide customers and employees with efficient, speedy, hassle-free service?

Working alone or with a small group, jot down as many ideas as possible without regard for whether they are practical or immediately usable. Then review all ideas for possible adoption in your organization. Put a check mark next to the ones you want to try.

❑ _____

❑ _____

❑ _____

❑ _____

❑ _____

❑ _____

❑ _____

❑ _____

❑ _____

❑ _____

❑ _____

❑ _____

❑ _____

❑ _____

❑ _____

❑ _____

❑ _____

Develop a priority list indicating when you will apply each selected idea. Describe tasks necessary to enact the A-Plus ideas (what is needed, who will initiate, etc.).

# Make Things Easier

Use this form to generate possible A-Plus convenience ideas as discussed in Chapter 8. How might your organization make life easier for customers and employees? What kinds of things are too time-consuming, unnecessarily repetitive, or cumbersome for people?

Working alone or with a small group, jot down as many ideas as possible without regard for whether they are practical or immediately usable. Then review all ideas for possible adoption in your organization. Put a check mark next to the ones you want to try.

❏ _____

❏ _____

❏ _____

❏ _____

❏ _____

❏ _____

❏ _____

❏ _____

❏ _____

❏ _____

❏ _____

❏ _____

❏ _____

❏ _____

❏ _____

❏ _____

Develop a priority list indicating when you will apply each selected idea. Describe tasks necessary to enact the A-Plus ideas (what is needed, who will initiate, etc.).

# Simplify Products

Use this form to generate possible A-Plus convenience ideas for simplifying your products or services. How might your organization make your products easier to use or your services more user-friendly for customers and employees?

Working alone or with a small group, jot down as many ideas as possible without regard for whether they are practical or immediately usable. Then review all ideas for possible adoption in your organization. Put a check mark next to the ones you want to try.

❑ _____

❑ _____

❑ _____

❑ _____

❑ _____

❑ _____

❑ _____

❑ _____

❑ _____

❑ _____

❑ _____

❑ _____

❑ _____

❑ _____

❑ _____

❑ _____

Develop a priority list indicating when you will apply each selected idea. Describe tasks necessary to enact the A-Plus ideas (what is needed, who will initiate, etc.).

*A-Plus Worksheets © 2004 Paul R. Timm. May be copied as needed for organizational use.*

# Notes and Ideas for Building Allegiance . . .

*A-Plus Worksheets © 2004 Paul R. Timm. May be copied as needed for organizational use.*

*A-Plus Worksheets © 2004 Paul R. Timm. May be copied as needed for organizational use.*